HOUSE CALLS

by
Patch Adams, M.D.

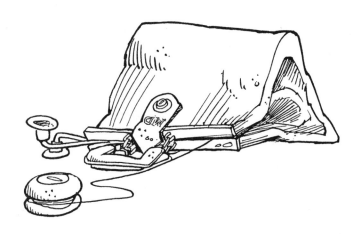

Robert D. Reed Publishers • San Francisco, California

Robert D. Reed Publishers

750 La Playa, Suite 647
San Francisco, CA 94121
Phone: 650/994-6570 • Fax: -6579
E-mail: 4bobreed@msn.com
http://www.rdrpublishers.com

Cartoonist and Cover Artist: **Jerry Van Amerongen**

Editor and Typesetter: **Pamela D. Jacobs, M.A.**

Assistant Editor: **Ann Jacobs**

Proofreader: **Paul Azevedo**

Cover Computer Graphics by: **Julia A. Gaskill**

at Graphics Plus

I **Library of Congress Cataloging-in-Publication Data**

Adams, Patch, 1945-
  House calls: how we can all heal the world one visit at a time /
  by Patch Adams, M.D.; cartoons by Jerry Van Amerongen;
  foreword by Robin Williams; editing by Pamela D. Jacobs, M.A.
          p.   cm.
Includes bibliographical references
ISBN 1-885003-18-8 (pbk.)
1. Hospital patients--Caricatures and cartoons.
2. Sick--Caricatures and cartoons.
3. Health--Caricatures and cartoons.
RA965.6.A23   1998
613--dc21   98-34266
                                          CIP
Manufactured, Typeset, and Printed in the United States of America

Note

This book is sold with the understanding that the subject matter covered herein is of a general nature and does not constitute medical, legal, or other professional advice for any specific individual or situation. Readers planning to take action in any of the areas that this book describes should seek professional advice from their doctors, specialists, and other advisers, as would be prudent and advisable under their given circumstances.

Contents

Foreword vi
Author's Acknowledgments viii
Introduction ix

Thoughts on Being Well 2
- Faith 4
- Love 9
- Humor 14
- Wonder 19
- Curiosity 24
- Creativity 29
- Nature 34
- Relaxation 39
- Community 44
- Passion 46
- Exercise 51
- Hope 56
- Imagination 58
- Peace 63
- Family 68
- Service 73
- Friendship 74
- Nutrition 76
- Wisdom 81
- Sense of Self 84

Things A Visitor Can Do 90
- Friendliness 92
- Relax 90
- Be A Good Listener 93
- Share Your Tenderness (in Your Own Way) 94
- More Thoughts on Sharing 95
- Be Part of a Healing Team 96
- Power Objects and Photos 98
- Touch 100
- What Can You Do For Them? 102
- Fun, Play, and Laughter 104
- Faith 106
- Listening 107

How To Be A Good Hospital Patient   108

Special Concerns When Visiting...   116
  – Children   116
  – Teenagers   118
  – The Elderly   119
  – The Mentally Ill   121
  – The Disabled   122
  – Dying Patients   124

Beginning   126

Bibliography   129

Health Resources   158

About The Cartoonist   160

About The Author   161

Foreword

by Robin Williams

A man visits his doctor and says, "Doc, my elbow hurts.
  What can I do?"
The doctor slams his foot down on the patient's toes.
"Owwww! Hey, what did you do that for?"
The doctor asks, "Do you still feel the pain in your elbow?"
"No."
"Next."

Does this seem like the way your physician treats you? Okay,
maybe your doctor doesn't stomp on your toes, but does he or she
ever seem impersonal or uncaring? Then maybe your doctor needs
to have a look at this book.

Patch Adams recommends that you can help maintain your
health with joy, laughter, and kindness. This is going to wreak
havoc in the health care industry because those things aren't
covered by your HMO. Patch also suggests that sometimes the
most helpful treatment is hope, love, relaxation, and the simple joy
of living. Wait until the pharmaceutical companies get a load of
this! Their blood pressure is going to go through the roof. He
doesn't recommend putting any of those things in a pill! It's radical!
It's anarchy!

Who knows? Maybe, as you read this, some scientists are
in a lab trying to design a pill that induces human kindness. Take
two pills every six hours and you'll help a friend in need, act
neighborly to a stranger, and cheer up the ill. The pharmaceutical
companies will tell us that it'll be a revolutionary drug that humanity
won't be able to live without. Don't fall for it!

Instead, read this book. It's filled with good, honest, common sense. For some, it will be an epiphany. Even if you're not ill, this book offers positive ways to lead life. Hopefully, it will affect those who need this information the most: the medical community.

Helping the infirm means more than just treating their maladies. It means offering them humor, compassion, and friendship. The insights in this book come from years of experience. Patch writes from the heart. He cares. And he won't stomp on your toes.

Author's Acknowledgments

To my performance partner, Susan Parenti, who has brought great breadth to my performing self. Her intelligence, creativity, and clarity toward social change has made me a much better instrument for change.

To Kathy Blomquist, Heidi Read, and Blair Voyvodic, M.D., who are making it possible for Gesundheit Institute to stand on its own. Then love, commitment, and intelligence have freed me and Gesundheit to emerge as a collective dream.

To Zag and Lars, my sons who help inspire me to make efforts for a peaceful world and who fill me with their love.

To Bowen, Beach Clown, Johnushka, Jan, Marina, and Maria, and all the clowns who play with me.

And to Jerry Van Amerongen, a brilliant cartoonist who teaches the celebration of human diversity through humor, for honoring me by making this book such a feast.

Introduction

by Patch Adams, M.D.

A quarter century in medicine has taught me that people who visit patients in the hospital do not know how to make the most of the visit, both for the patient and for themselves. Yet hospital visits can bring back the potent healing we have lost with the disappearance of old-fashioned house calls. Visits can be easy and fun. Anyone can do it. You don't need a degree or license.

A hospital stay is a vulnerable situation. Patients and their families have been (often suddenly) placed in a situation of unknowns where fears and confusion make most people anxious and stressed. Lives are disrupted or even changed forever.

Few things can enhance a hospital stay as much as a visit from a friend, who can bring love, empathy, and even play to calm these anxieties. When I interview patients about their hospital stays, consistently they say the most powerful element in making their time more pleasant is the presence of a friend.

I have asked patients what qualities of the person or visit are most important to their well-being. For most, simply having a friend visit is of paramount importance, especially if the hospital stay is long. Showing up is a giant step.

Patients speak of the importance of love, humor, and joy in transforming their hospital experience. Empathy and being spoiled (cared for) make a difference. If they feel at ease with it, visitors can share the comforting tradition of a patient's faith, thereby creating a huge refuge from suffering. Stories, photos, mementoes, and games can all be tools for a healing hospital visit, too.

What I have heard described as the "potency of a visiting friend" involves the same qualities that make up a good health professional's "bedside manner." In the history of medicine, bedside manner reached its zenith with the house call.

Why House Calls?

For 28 years I have made house calls. I feel that I could not have been a family doctor without them. For the curious who love people, house calls are a doorway to enchantment.

Imagine yourself as one of my patients. When I visit you at home, I try to look at and examine everything. I ask many questions. I like to see how everything works when you're in your home— which is, hopefully, your sanctuary. I want to know what each object is doing in your life. I'm looking for people or things to call into play to help relieve suffering and expand understanding.

I love to be with a new family and explore the many complex factors which make up their human community. No two families and no two house calls are alike. Each time I hope the children of the home will invite me into their room, their world. I note every interest. I work and play with getting close, hoping to build trust so the kids will know they can count on me as a friend and a doctor.

Clowning around creates the context for each house call. Sometimes I am invited for dinner (what a bonus!). Beyond my role as doctor, each visit helps me as a person; for I, too, feel comforted, loved, and respected in this relationship. House calls help the physician and the patient access the healing power of intimacy which friends and family already know well. They can do the same for you!

Reviving House Calls?

When medicine left the service sector to thrive in the business world, the house call was dropped as "impractical." As technological medicine began to dominate the practice of medicine, the house call was discarded. The process of bringing care to patients was reversed.

I think that the loss of the house call has been the biggest blow to the art of medicine in this century. Not only has the patient lost this precious attention, but the physician has not found a replacement for the lost intimacy that in a hospital setting is crucial to burnout prevention. I believe this loss of intimacy also parallels the rise in malpractice cases, especially as we have begun to treat the doctor/patient interaction as a business contract, not a friendship.

Hospitals, as hard as the staff may try, have not been comforting places. When I visit hospitals, no one looks as if they feel at home or want to be there. Staff, patient, and visitor all feel and act as if they are in strange territory. I chose to name this book and visitor kit *House Calls* to rekindle that deep meaning the house call brought to human interaction. My hope and premise are that most of what was of value in the house call—for the doctor, the patient, and the family alike—can be recreated in a hospital through the visitor's intention to do so.

Using The Mind-Body Connection

In the past 25 years, medicine has been defining the field of psychoneuroimmunology—known to the lay public as the mind-body connection. We have come to understand that stresses (physical, mental, and spiritual) have an effect on the body's biochemistry and physiology. The body is made up of many systems and what happens in one or more affects all the rest in some way. This deep, interactive connection goes way beyond the "hip bone connected to the thigh bone."

Extensive studies have found that over long periods of time, nourishing elements—such as love, humor, wonder, curiosity, passion, forgiveness, giving, sharing, hope, enthusiasm, and joy—stimulate the immune system. They help our bodies fight infection and stimulate natural killer cells that fight cancer and affect the general way we care about and for ourselves and others.

Conversely, when anger, resentment, ambivalence, guilt, boredom, loneliness, and fear are held for a long time, they can suppress our natural protective systems and make us feel worse. The emotions themselves do not cause the problems. Problems are caused when we hold onto emotions for hours, days, or even years. Express each emotion as it comes up. However, do not nurture or prolong the emotions that may hurt you.

It is important to note that each person is as unique biochemically as he or she is in physical appearance. How the biochemical processes will manifest in each person remains to be seen. Health professionals in the field of preventive medicine do not want to wait for the consequences. Instead, they suggest that living a happy, vibrant life is essential for well-being.

Visitor As Good Medicine

Taking these things into consideration, from my point of view as a physician, I believe that how you visit a patient goes beyond friend visiting friend. It is bringing strong medicine to the bedside. Inherent in the visit is actual involvement in the healing of the patient and the relief of suffering. Plus, it is good for the visitor.

Please do not be hurt if a patient cannot or asks not to have a visitor. Notify a family member of your interest in visiting whenever he or she is ready for company. Larry Dossey, M.D. has convincingly shown in his book, *Healing Words*, that prayer at a distance has measurable healing qualities. So when you cannot be with a patient, friend, or a loved one, you may pray for that person if you wish.

Healing Our World

This book, *House Calls*, is a "visitor's kit" that was originally designed for visiting hospital patients. However, now I realize that the information can be just as useful in visiting friends in nursing homes, prisons, or any place where people may be suffering and wishing they were elsewhere.

If you share my concern that hospitals, nursing homes, prisons, etc. are not ideal environments for people of any kind, I suggest that you share the healing behaviors you practice with patients and friends with every other patient, visitor, and employee of these institutions to boost the health of the whole environment.

If you can stretch yourself to see the great medical value of your "house call" to your friend and others in the institution, then why not make another leap? Surely, the general population exhibits in many ways its need for tender and fun encounters. Realize that the way you treat any ailing friend is a powerful tool at your disposal. Offering your same friendly personality to the world at large will make it a better place for all. This book, *House Calls*, offers simple ways for all citizens to improve the health of their society.

Healing Our World

House Calls has a short segment on how to be a patient in a hospital. One juicy portion of this book ("kit") addresses the many different opportunities that we have for improving our health and wellness in the mind-body model. I will show you how to use toys suggested in the hospital visitor kit, and I will suggest other implements of delight that you might develop on your own. You will find references for further study and exploration in each section.

It is a great honor to create a book with Jerry Van Amerongen. Working with this master of humor in the human condition has been one of my fondest fantasies realized. So much of making a house call to a patient, friend, or the world is doing so in the context of fun, humor, and play. What Jerry and I want to communicate is important (formerly classified as "serious"). We want you to have fun with all of your human interactions, especially during vulnerable moments.

I want patients everywhere to benefit from your house calls. So go out there and help heal the world one visit at a time.

THOUGHTS ON BEING WELL

Few things get a person more interested in being healthy than a big bout of being sick. When I was in medical school there was no vision taught for being well. No professor ever spoke of what being healthy was. The most common thing said was, "Health is the absence of disease."

I wanted a definition that could fit all ages and situations. I wanted a way for people with cancer, or who are paralyzed, to see themselves as healthy. I define "health" as "a happy, vibrant life, doing the most with what you have, with delight. Using this criteria, I have found healthy people from all walks of life.

My most important teachers of health have been elderly people who, on examination, seem to have every disease in the textbook of internal medicine, but they act healthy.

In speaking with healthy people, they describe things that are important to their well-being. Some people feel healthy by focusing primarily on the ways they are healthy, not the ways they are sick. Other people see their sickness as an opportunity for growth and learning. Why not explore the effects of each on your quality of life? Each has the capacity to alter pain and suffering.

When you visit your sick friend, explore these things with them where you are comfortable. I encourage patients to explore these ideas with all who visit. A lot comes up in candid conversation at these vulnerable times that can help all involved.

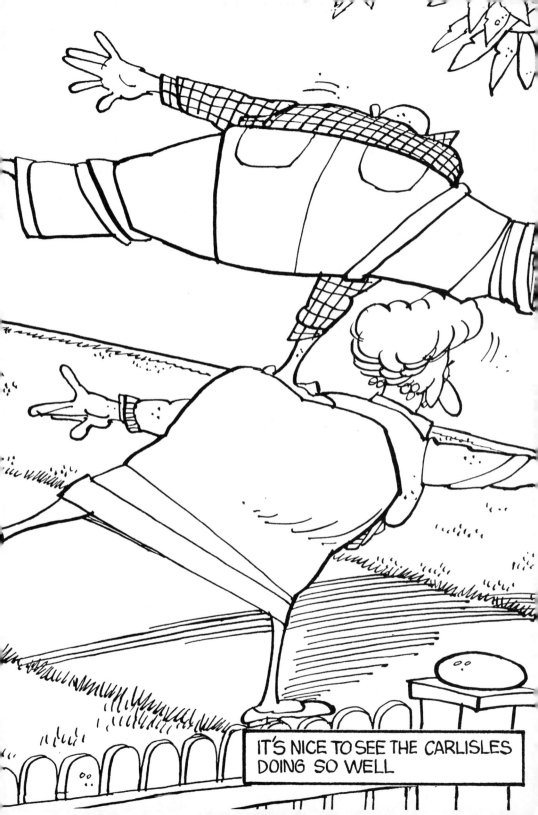

Faith

Faith can have a profound impact on health. It is a very personal experience of thought and surrender, which can comfort in every situation. Faith only requires that one fully embrace possibility. One doesn't have to do anything else in order to receive the benefits. Faith is free and available to all people at all times. One can reap the same benefits, whether it's a faith based on religion, or on fishing or music. The value is in the depth of the embrace.

Things To Do:

1. Think of all the things in which you feel a "**special magic**." Single out one and focus on it for a long time. Get clear about the ways in which your life has been better for this faith. Ask the patient, "What is magic for you?" Ask for details. And share your own ideas.

"Special Magic" means different things to different people.

2. Feel gratitude for living and show it through your actions.

Stephen is grateful for his commute.

3. Help others who suffer.

Gloria needs help moving in harmony with others.

4. Be optimistic as a general habit. Cheerleading costumes are ideal.

Love

"You only have to let the soft animal of your body love what it loves."
                                                              – Mary Oliver

Love has an enormous impact on how one feels and acts. There are so many kinds of love and within each is the capacity to help our health: within each, supreme heights of good feelings.

There is love of a partner, and no matter how many songs or poems of love are written, there will still be a whole lot more to say. There is friendship's love, a thread that can connect and enliven your whole life. So can the love of God or nature; the love of arts, and rubber bands, and tapioca pudding (the lumps); dancing, discovery, bicycles. Love invites itself into every aspect of life where it is welcomed. And one love increases the possibility of another. Try to be wide open and ready.

Things To Do:

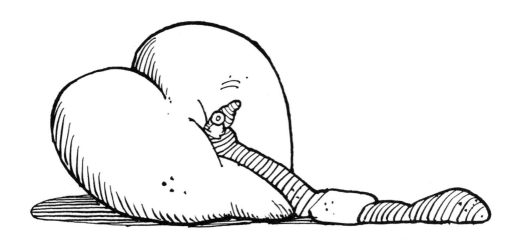

1. Take a close look at the part that "love" plays in your life. Make an inventory of love: people, things, ideas, experiences. Try to live your gratitude.

2. If you're visiting a patient whom you love in any way, please find ways to share that love with him or her. Twinkly eyes, smiles and touch are starters. Every patient needs love and so do you.

3. As the visitor, feel how good it feels to have been able to relieve suffering by your visit. You did that!

4. Now try that love on everyone else. Get to know everyone, and spend time with someone who is feeling hurt or lonely.

Humor

"The purpose of the doctor is to entertain the patient while the disease takes its course."
                                                        – Voltaire

There is a reason for the phrase "comic relief." When suffering is great, there is a call for relief. Whatever we are nervous about or emotional over is where jokes come from. And yet, in a hospital, where people are suffering greatly, one wonders when humor is appropriate.

Clowning in hospitals has convinced me that you can even take humor to a death bed. Imagine if you are the sick person and all your experience with your visitors is gloominess, even doom for your life. Is that the way you want to spend your hospital stay? Is that the way you want to die?

One alternative is to bring humor to the hospital – and to the world, which seems to be suffering as well.

"Life doesn't cease to be funny when people die, any more than it ceases to be serious when people laugh."
                                                        – George Bernard Shaw

Things To Do:

1. Decide to be silly as a way of life. Now go do it. You'll want to do a thousand experiments. And then a thousand more.

2. Do funny, for funny's sake. Don't evaluate its success on the basis of laughter. Simply do the things and watch reactions. Keep what works.

3. Walk around the ward clucking like a chicken. Flap your wings. Lay an egg in the nursing station.

4. Encourage visitors and patients to serenade other visitors or patients in the waiting room. It's amazing how little it takes to inspire a chuckle. For example, mismatched socks can pay rich dividends. And just the expectation of a giggle is infectious.

Wonder

"When it's over, I want to say all my life I was a bride married to amazement."
                                                        – Mary Oliver

Woooooo! Pop your eye out! Stay amazed every day, for the sunrise and the sunset. Try to be present in each moment through the gifts of your senses. Smell things. Look carefully. Touch everything. Let all those things and more live in your memory, and let them dart in and out of your imagination. It's impossible to be amazed and bored at the same time. Open wide!

Things To Do:

1. Go camping in nature. Spend your time watching, touching, listening to, and smelling everything. See if you can focus on only one sound or scent. Take a magnifying glass and carefully investigate one square yard anywhere.

2. Walk or ride around the hospital ward and feel the complexity of everything. Watch how it operates. Look for details. If you can, try collecting stories of patients and staff to get a closer look at the hospital as an "organism." See how the various types of personalities affect the environment. What types of things does the staff do to help others? Be observant.

3. When I am ill and have to stay indoors for a long time, I love to look at nature books. Think of something that you have always been interested in but haven't had the time to explore. Use the illness as your opportunity. Engage your visitors in your interests. Make up skits you can all do.

"Really fellas, we'll all play 'Little Bo Peep.' It'll be fun!"

4. If all else fails, study your feet or knees. Appreciate how they're one hell of a design!

Curiosity

"Hey daddy, what dat dere?
And what dat unner der?
And daddy, oh hey daddy, hey what day say up dere?"

– Oscar Brown, Jr.

In all my years of clowning, I have been awed by the power of curiosity to relieve suffering. I hold up a sack of things to a patient in pain and they're waiting to know what is in it relieves pain. Maybe it is the curiosity in the asking of the questions about life that makes philosophers out of everyone. Some subjects (such as love, life, death, and meaning) inspire curiosity almost every time they are spoken.

Things To Do:

1. See what would happen if you walked backwards (carefully), chirping like a bird.

2. Give a wrapped present in a wrapped box in another wrapped box, and another wrapped box. Each level can be filled with surprises — such as photographs, memorabilia, treats, or art. Use creative or recycled wrapping.

Curiosity gets the best of Curtis.

3. Read books and articles about your ailment (or those of your loved one). Study the subject. Learn how complementary medicine can be helpful. Study anatomy books until you feel amazed and privileged to have such a body.

4. If a friend or loved one has a long-lasting illness, consider making costumes of the affected organ and creating a performance with friends and the patient. For example, how about a singing quartet called "The Liverettes"?

The Crawley's have a friend with a troublesome toe.

Creativity

Everyone has creative potential. "Creativity" involves using your imagination and inventiveness. Your unique expression of yourself is your creativity. Whether it is the way you walk, wash dishes, or say "hello"—everything you do is your performance of creative expression.

Creativity can be magic when visiting people who are ill. Patients are generally happy to see visitors. At this vulnerable time, they are thankful for your efforts and attention. It's a grand time to be creative and go to extremes.

Things To Do:

1. Hospital food can be less than desirable. Working within the patient's dietary limitations, bring in some favorite meals. You may want to wear a butler's costume or a pizza delivery outfit. Bringing in really nutritious food is an added bonus.

2. Singing get well cards can be fun. Go to the trouble to have a costume or two handy. Occasionally, visit a thrift store to find just the right get-up.

3. Bring in a group of friends to have an "unbirthday" party, a play reading, a flycasting class, or anything you can think up.

4. I have to put in a plug here for clowning. Goofy visits are appreciated all over the world. You can put together a clown costume and use it all of your life to creatively cheer up people. Start with visits to nursing homes.

Nature

"Nature fills your lap with pleasures all her own."
                    – William Wordsworth

Nature is powerful medicine. Never let yourself get bored with nature. Appreciate every tree, bird, or sunset. Feeling the miracle of life through interaction with nature can be essential for your good health. Pets and gardens have been found to be beneficial for health. In fact, there are formal therapies using each. Watching a fish tank and listening to moving water have both been shown to lower blood pressure. When patients can view natural scenery from their beds, they fare better. Of all the things given to cheer up the sick, flowers reign supreme.

Things To Do:

1. Flowers are always healing for people who are ill, unless they are allergic... Achoo!

2. Look around the hospital for gardens where you can go with the patient, even if you need to borrow a wheelchair.

3. Remember, we are human nature. Take delight in studying our nature. There is much humor awaiting you.

Bob continually studies human nature.

4. Some hospitals will let you bring a special pet for a visit. This can really lift spirits.

Relaxation

"Don't sweat the small stuff. It's all small stuff."

When in doubt, relax. Be cool. Don't worry, be happy. Breathe in slowly, breathe out slowly. Think sweet thoughts. Think of your blessings. Hang loose. Melt in the presence of your friends. Pray, sing, and make weird noises. Laugh for long periods of time. Hug for a long time. Get and give massages. Give up guilt, hate, duty, sacrifice, boredom, loneliness, fear, judgment, and formality. Plop down on a big pillow. Say nice things to yourself and to others.

Stress and anxiety are harmful to people who cannot relax. Try practicing various relaxation techniques.

Things To Do:

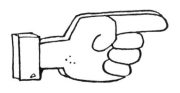

1. Notice how often just having a good conversation and listening to a patient or friend relaxes both of you.

2. Just showing up can help a troubled friend relax.

3. Go for a walk and linger where you wish. Stop and smell the roses.

4. Listen to your favorite music. Water your plants. And play with your children.

Community

Extensive studies confirm that having a strong sense of community and its support to you can be a major factor in the recovery from a heart attack. By "community," I don't mean a location on a map (although that's a community, too). Here I am referring to a sense of belonging to at least one group of people. This could be a church group, a civic organization, or a bowling league. A community could include people who go to the same corner grocery store.

Throughout most of human history, a community was a tribe and later a village. Initially, community offered protection, safety, and insurance against any threats that came along. Today, in the absence of tribal communities, many people must be responsible for their own security. I think that our society's high level of anxiety is mainly due to this loss of belonging.

If you have good friends, you are well on your way to building community. Nurturing these connections is good for your health, and a gift to Gaia. I think human survival depends on our developing a global community—and quickly.

Things To Do:

1. Make a list of every group to which you have belonged. Write something about that association. Add to your list the various communities which you encounter each day (such as all of the people who use the toll booth, bank at your bank, have season tickets to anything, subscribe to a magazine, or own a particular model of car). There must be 10,000 of them in your life. Notice the number of people with whom you stand on common ground.

2. Study a community, such as a hospital ward. Walk around, ask questions, offer to help, and talk to lonely or scared patients. Interview people who clean the ward. Notice the impact of various health care professionals. Spread good cheer.

3. From your experience in life, what factors seem to increase a sense of community? Observe your interactions with others. What could be done in each of these encounters (however casual) to enhance community? What inhibits your doing it?

4. One great way to understand community is to create one and stay involved with it for at least ten years, although any amount of time will be of value. For example, how about creating a local chapter of "The Society For People Who Enjoy Sunsets"?

Passion

"The secret of life is to have a task. Something that you devote your entire life to, something to bring everything to, every minute of the day for your whole life. And the important thing is, it must be something you can't possibly do."

– Henry Moore

Passion is the thoughts and feelings for something that has an irresistible hold on you. You cannot imagine your life without it. It is hard to tell if it consumes you or you it. Though it is very intense, it does not hurt because it is something you want. It is essential to have passion based on love, not power, or a passion can cause damage.

A hobby, a friendship, or an idea... indeed, every part of life may be approached with passion. Many people who get sick put their passions aside "until they get better." I have noticed often those who continue their passions through illness, especially chronic illness, seem to recover more quickly and resume their lives more fully. They inspire others. One of my favorite explorations is trying to discover another person's passions. Try to share your friends' passions.

Things To Do:

1. Think of your whole life. Whew! Wow! What have you felt passion for? How has it changed over time? Notice the many ways in which passion has come into your life. What hobbies have you enjoyed? What sports? Have some of your passions remained constant?

Bob's wife now intercepts all magazines and brochures dealing with fish or fishing.

2. Create a new passion. Over the next month, search for and find something (an idea, a person, or a place) with which to get involved. Study it, talk with many people about it, and write to others who are interested in it.

Phil's well on his way to creating a new passion.

3. Think of a friend. Think of something special you could do for him or her. Go to extremes. Feel yourself driven by your love for this person. Do things for the thrill of doing them.

"I thought when I included you,
you would at least bring the mixed nuts."

4. Think up a fun way to introduce one of your passions to a patient in the hospital. Do a performance, give a slide show, sing an opera, or show off your Zippo lighter collection.

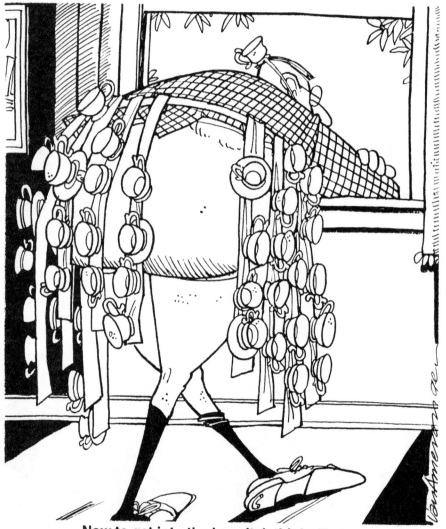

Now to get into the hospital, thinks Ted.

Exercise

Use it or lose it!

Exercise is so important that I wish it were required. Everything is better if you are fit. Fitness is just as valuable if you have some disability. There are strength exercises such as push-ups and weights. There are endurance exercises such as running and cycling (and, of course, walking). And there are flexibility exercises such as yoga. There is no getting around the time you must invest in fitness. It is hard to be a pessimist when you are a regular exerciser. When you exercise, you declare a future by investing your time and effort. Any exercise is a giant step.

Things To Do:

1. All right—you're in bed in the hospital. Move everything you can, as much as you can. If you can get up and walk—do so. Pretend you're doing the tango with the crash cart. You could claim that you have strange spasms. Writhe in bed.

2. Take stairs, not elevators. For the advanced, do the above while saying "werble" (hold the ___ sound) and (then) splout!

3. Run forward and backward in place. It actually feels the same. Try it for 10 minutes each way.

For a moment, Raymond didn't realize
his wife was running in place.

4. For the reading fanatic, a stationary bike with a book rack provides guaranteed reading time each day.

Hope

"Hope is a thing with feathers that perches in the soul..."
– Emily Dickinson

Visitors can bring massive quantities of hope to sick friends or loved ones. Remember, whatever forecasts you may hear regarding a patient's future (however gloomy), are only gambler's odds. Think of how many millions of people play the Lottery even though the odds are millions to one. Everyone is hoping for a miracle and a winning ticket. In the medical world, many doctors have seen amazing healing miracles in their practices. So always remain hopeful.

Maybe hope shows us that there is a big mystery over which we have no control. Sometimes our hope is for a cure; sometimes it is simply for diminished suffering. Please, if you are feeling pessimistic or whiny, do not make that evident in your visit. An uplifting attitude is more beneficial than you realize.

Things To Do:

1. Before visiting the patient, practice having hope for big things such as world peace, a clean environment, and cherished diversity. When you are full of hope, go in the door.

2. Every day, hope for something that you know can happen because of your effort and proceed to do it.

3. Go throughout the ward offering hope to others. Remember, a patient once up and able to walk, becomes another patient's potential visitor, so everything here applies to patients who are getting well, too.

4. Decide that hope is going to be an essential part of your life in every moment. Treasure the cockeyed optimist. Don't call for an eye doctor!

Imagination

"Imagination is more important than knowledge."
                                    – Albert Einstein

Imagination is an infinite resource that cannot be diminished by overuse or underuse. If you say, "Oh, I have no imagination..." then you have an enormous treat in store when you recognize this powerful tool that you were born with. <u>Everyone</u> has one! Every thought, daydream, and dream is a sign that your imagination is alive and well.

Imagination is the ultimate playmate. It goes anywhere and does anything with you at no cost. The only limit is time. Most of your imagination never leaves your head in the form of actions; yet your imagination can stimulate action. I think imagination is the most complicated gift life has to offer. We never touch a fraction of our imagination potential. We have to bury it in order to be bored. Someone who imagines there is nothing to do or to be, still has a big imagination. It is the one place where everything is possible, right now. Use your imagination with passion.

Things To Do:

1. Next time you are caught in traffic or laid up in bed, imagine things. What if chlorophyll in plants were orange instead of green? What if we had five arms around our shoulders? How would that affect hugging?

2. Think about how your life, community, and society influence your imagination. How are your likes and dislikes influenced by the media? Flex your imagination beyond any constraints. <u>You</u> are in the driver's seat.

Gary's imagination is easily swayed by his environment.

3. What triggers your imagination to run wild? How can you turn on your imagination? What activities help trigger it? I think that television has crippled the dimensions of our imaginations. Turn off your TV. Turn up your imagination.

4. Take a new interest to an extreme. Laugh often with crazed laughter.

Rusty's life took a dark turn when Ted bought "The Big Book of Fishermen's Knots."

Peace

I wonder what world peace would feel like. It's the only thing mentioned here that no one has ever experienced. It requires an agreement among all people not to hurt each other. Each of us can try to live in peace in our daily life. By intentionally relating to others in positive ways, we can increase the possibility of peace. In my experience, people who are peaceful generate a more peaceful environment. That is why I love clowning; it transforms the environment. Toddlers do the same thing.

World peace starts within each of us. Having inner peace can lower your blood pressure and relieve stress. It also helps to lower the stress level and blood pressure of others around you.

When we achieve peace we will experience a more creative, cooperative, and dynamic state that will improve our health. It will take all of us working together to achieve peace. So each person can participate and work toward this important goal.

Things To Do:

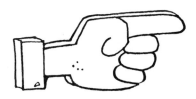

1. As a visitor be prepared to listen and to sit acceptingly with all the pain, anger, and sadness the patient or his or her family is feeling. Be calm, have patience, and show a desire to help.

2. If you sing or play an instrument, or have any kind of interest, you might offer to come in and do something for patients. It's the friendly showing up that is so important. It adds life and peacefulness.

3. Be gracious, kind, and demonstratively thankful. Do something to show your appreciation to the hospital staff. They are probably overworked and do not have the time to hang out with patients as they may dream of doing.

4. While the patient is in the hospital, please do not bring in fights, arguments, or problems. Try to resolve problems yourself or work them out with friends. Compassion and kindness are called for here.

Family

"Home is where you go and they have to take you in."
                                              – Robert Frost

A "family" is made up of people who love you and people whom
you can love. This can include a nuclear family, an extended
family, your family of friends, and even the family of humankind.
All families offer the potential for tenderness and security.

The fact that you are related does not guarantee that you will
have deep family feelings for each other. Relatives offer you the
opportunity to strive for closer ties. If you do not have strong
family connections with your own relatives, search elsewhere.
There are many potential families waiting for you. Maintain as
many close family ties as possible.

Things To Do:

1. Look closely at your different types of families. Study their
histories and biographies. Look up at least two relatives and old
friends whom you haven't seen for some time. Feel the evolution
of families; it is the river of life. A family is a mirror that helps
us to understand ourselves. A family can inspire and fuel our
life's work. When we need a haven, it is the family.

THE BELLAMY BROTHERS REMAIN CLOSE

2. Call up every family member (whatever family it may be) today. Catch up with them and thank them for being in your life.

3. Develop a constant feeling of delight in being in the family of woman and man. You will know you are there when you no longer feel like a stranger and you always feel at home. Every day, imagine a world full of this universal love of all people. This was well described by the poet, Walt Whitman. Find an example in his work.

Along about mid-week the Swensen family likes to shake things up.

4. I love it when some people are asked if they have a family and they respond, "Sure, I have two cats." Could the plants in your garden be your family? Surely I have met people whose car or truck is their family. What is in your family? Your yard flamingo flock?

Service

"Only a life lived for others is worthwhile."
— Albert Einstein

Few things are as strong a medicine for the soul as the giving of your time to help others and nature. It is amazing how often I hear doctors and nurses (who volunteer at free clinics here in the United States or travel to poor countries to provide free health care) say it is the most rewarding work they do.

A mother's life is devoted to service. I am not speaking of acts done out of duty or obligation. I am talking about helping others for the sheer pleasure of giving. Joyful service is its own reward; it sustains the giver and the receiver.

Things To Do:

1. Be friendly to everyone, whether you are a patient or a visitor. Friendliness creates the best atmosphere for healing and it feels good, too.

2. Offer to rub the shoulders of the cleaning staff or nurses to thank them for working so hard for you and your loved ones.

3. Go to other rooms to visit other patients. Strike up a new friendship. Help turn the environment into a community. When you can, visit nursing homes and bring your warmth, humor, and compassion to the people there.

4. Look throughout your community and find where there is need or suffering. Offer ways to help others using your talents.

Friendship

"You are my mirror
in your eyes I float
my reality proven

> *I dwell*
> *in you*
> *and so*
> *I know*
> *I am."*

"You Are"   – May Swenson

For most people, their friends are the most important part of their lives. There is no close second. As a physician, I have noticed that the most pain is associated with loneliness. People need mutual love among friends in order to be healthy. The absence of friendship is strongly related to illness and violence.

Begin by loving yourself so you can understand others loving you. I like how the thing between friends is called friendship. To guide a ship requires lots of attention to detail by one's actions.

Things To Do:

1. Be a friend to yourself. Ten minutes each day gossip to yourself about what a nice person you are. Kiss a mirror!

2. Think of your friends. Write each of them a card and thank them for loving you. Include a "gosh!" or a "gee whiz!"

3. Try spending a week acting as if everyone is your friend. Watch yourself be friendly. Go to extremes. I like standing on an active street corner, waving and saying "hello."

4. Think of things that you have a friend relationship to: your pickup truck, a favorite coffee mug, or a particular hat. Strike up a conversation with it and speak its part. When you perfect this, do it in public.

Alternate The Following To Build Friendships:

1. If you want to become friends with people, learn as much as you can about them. Try out their interests. Share your deepest feelings freely. Listen to their dreams and make them yours in every way possible. Give them the gift of being truly known.

2. Preserve friendships with time shared. Long-distance friendships can be nourished with letters, phone calls, and e-mail.

3. Surround yourself at home and at work with pictures and reminders of your friends. They are icons for the soul.

4. Give friends shelter and support. Move from the insurance of cash to the insurance of clan.

5. Play with your friends every time you are together.

Nutrition

Clearly, eating a balanced vegetarian/macrobiotic diet is the most nutritious diet that most people could follow. So much of our diet is not nutritious. Eat fruits and vegetables for snacks. Drink a lot more water. Lots more. Any step toward fresh, whole foods and away from processed foods is great. Cutting back on sugar, salt, and fats are each important steps.

Learning to cook can often make foods you did not like become some that you do like. Be tickled over each small step such as switching from white rice to brown. For most people, just eating less is beneficial.

Things To Do:

1. Find out what the patient is allowed to eat and then bring in picnics for him or her. While it is best to bring nutritious food, sometimes special treats may be all right. Food made with love has health benefits all its own. It is the gesture or ritual that matters.

The Yardly's practice food safety

2. Read some books and articles about nutrition. Learn why research is encouraging many people to become vegetarians.

Evidently the heat from the grill drew a good deal of oxygen from the air around Allen.

3. Bring fresh cut fruits and vegetables on platters for the staff and patients.

"It's disrespectful of fruit in general, Mr. Inkstrom,
and to Blueberries in particular."

4. Get involved with gardening—the creation of food. Bring your prized tomatoes with you to the hospital.

Wisdom

"Experience is not what happens to you, but what you do with what happens to you."

– Aldous Huxley

If wisdom's a diamond, experience is a diamond mine.

"Wisdom"—how appropriate that it sounds like a combination of "wise" and "dumb." Often, wisdom is knowing how dumb you are in the larger scheme of things. There is wisdom to make every part of life easier. For each person, wisdom desired and gained will be different.

The wisdom of others is available for the taking—whether from the Bible or Koran, a poem or political treatise, a cartoon or a piece of art. One expression of wisdom is the sharing of community and one experience of community is the sharing of wisdom. You can collect it every day.

The following poem by Mary Oliver contains great wisdom to offer patients. Here is a prescription for that vital, loving life—which research has shown to be a boon to your health and feeling of community.

When Death Comes

When death comes
like the hungry bear in autumn;
when death comes and takes all the bright coins from his purse

to buy me, and snaps the purse shut;
when death comes
like the measle-pox

when death comes
like an iceberg between the shoulder blades

I want to step through the door full of curiosity, wondering:
what is it going to be like, that cottage of darkness?

And therefore I look upon everything
as a brotherhood and a sisterhood,
and I look upon time as no more than an idea,
and I consider eternity as another possibility,

and I think of each life as a flower; as common
as a field daisy, and as singular;

and each name a comfortable music in the mouth,
tending, as all music does, toward silence,

and each body a lion of courage, and something
previous to the earth.

When it's over, I want to say: all my life
I was a bride married to amazement.
I was the bridegroom, taking the world into my arms.

When it's over, I don't want to wonder
if I have made of my life something particular and real.
I don't want to find myself sighing and frightened
or full of argument.

I don't want to end up simply having visited this world.

Things To Do:

1. Think of all of the information and ideas that you have that make up your wisdom. Look at your wisdom in human relationships. What would you advise a middle school class? Where do you want more wisdom?

Joyce calls it her "window of shared wisdom."

2. When you find some wisdom (from your lover, your doctor, or a book), write it on a 3x5 card and pin it up. Notice where your wisdom comes from.

3. Everyone has some wisdom that is in fact false. Look at some of your wisdom around you and your illness. Is your illness suggesting any change in wisdom as you understand it? Wisdom is evolutionary.

4. If you love conversation, explore the wisdom of whomever you are with, with interest and curiosity. Do this as often as you can with anyone. It will help move the world to an acceptance of diversity.

Sense of Self

One of the most important factors for good health is self-esteem; liking yourself in a friendly way and being glad you are you. If you did not get this from your parents or society, then listen to and accept the loving words of your friends. Believe that they are accurate in describing the you they know.

"No one
can be sure
by himself
of his own being."

                "You Are"   – May Swenson

If your parents and friends have reflected to you an understanding of your worth, <u>still</u> listen to the loving words of others. Believe! Be the person you want to be and work and play (hard) for your desires and needs. This is an opposite to selfish. There is a good chance if you love yourself you can relate to the cheer, "Yea Life!"

Things To Do:

1. Hang out with yourself and a mirror. Always look yourself in the eye for half an hour a day. Clothes on, clothes off, with make up, lots of faces ... YOU! Aren't you great?!

Mr. Chambers often imagines his activities are accompanied by a swell of heroic music

2. Look closely at your life (as the character George Bailey did in the movie "It's A Wonderful Life"). See where you have loved the you you were. Notice all you have created and imagine the world without you. If you feel you have not created very much, then go out there and follow your dreams—the real ones. See how much easier it is when you have people helping.

It's Nora Shipley Day over at Nora Shipley's.

3. The clown in me recommends: "Get a costume for the outrageous you and go spread joy. Visit nursing homes." Nothing can give you a strong sense of liking yourself as the service to others and to nature.

Phillip celebrates summer with an event of his own planning.

4. Have very intimate exchanges of your biographies with 100 people for at least 8 hours each. Ideally, spend half the time in one person's home and half the time in the other's home (or choose another place). Try out each other's interests. Please think of, and then be the you you want to be in each moment.

Casual comments regarding the pleasantness of his speaking voice, have resonated well with Allen.

...As opposed to the person who lacks a proper sense of self.

THINGS A VISITOR CAN DO

Visits of friends and colleagues can be a big boost to the patient's healthy connectedness to their community.

Anyone can help a friend through a hospital stay. The longer the stay, the more valuable the visits are. If your friend is ready to receive visitors, drop in when you can. Any visit can be strong medicine for the patient <u>and</u> <u>visitor</u>. For example, studies show that people who have a strong community of friends in their lives survive heart attacks best.

Research in mind-body-spirit medicine (psychoneuroim-munology) confirms the biochemistry and physiology that supports what poets, artists, mystics, and fools have always known—that love, compassion, humor, empathy, tenderness, faith, touch, creativity, and service all help people feel better. So any kind of visit is great when these qualities are expressed. Please avoid bringing in arguments or problems. Wait until the person is well or resolve the problems yourself.

The following section explores things that visitors may consider. Plan to make your visits fun and of value.

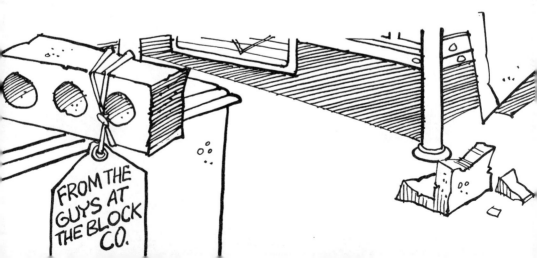

Friendliness

If one tossed compassion, love, humor, empathy, tenderness, faith, touch, creativity, and service all into one body and had to use a word for its expression, that word would be "friendliness."

Relax No matter what part of the body is lost or what strange color the skin has, this person is still your friend. Be natural (unless your natural way is grumpy or whiny). Feel at ease in the room. Ask if your friend needs anything.

Be a Good Listener   Often being a good listener is exactly
what is needed. Listen well when the patient shares the details
of the journey—fears, hopes, frustrations. Empathize by telling
some of your own story (show your scar).

Share Your Tenderness (in Your Own Way)   If the
patient is clearly your friend, then pour on your tenderness as
best you can. How you do this should suit *you*. A grandmother
quilter and a member of a motorcycle gang will probably act out
tenderness and friendliness differently. Think of ways the
patient means something to you, feel it as love and spread that
love in the visit as compassion.

More Thoughts on Sharing

Be Part of a Healing Team

If the hospital stay will be long, a lasting friendliness will be important. Try not to see the visit as an obligation or responsibility; rather see it as a privilege to be part of a healing team. Think of words such as pal, chum, mate, buddy, companion, playmate, and friend. Then *act*.

Power Objects and Photos

Both of my children were very attached to objects in their child-hood. The oldest was bonded to a blanket and the youngest to a teddy bear. As a physician I was amazed at the sedative and calming gifts the objects brought quickly and consistently to my sons. I could not think of a medication that brought that kind of serenity.

As the children aged I could see that there was pressure for them to detach from these objects. How often when I see adults reach for antidepressants or antianxiety medication, I wish they would reach for a teddy instead. Maybe to the bookworm a power object is a book and to the gardener, a straw hat.

Think about the patient you are visiting. What are his or her interests and hobbies? Can you think of a powerful memento? This could be an autographed baseball or a piece of music. The most common object is a photo—its content can soothe, trans-port, and represent the presence of loved ones or a precious memory.

Spiritual artifacts—a Buddha, a cross, or a feather—can be important. Patients often put up all their get well cards as a garland of protection, a paper embrace.

If the stay is long, rotate objects or bring in new ones.

Touch

Touch is essential for comfort. We could not have human community without it. Just think of how we use the word. A story that moves us emotionally is "touching," and the person moved is "touched." To contact persons or emotions, we get "in touch with" them. The phone company suggests that we call to "reach out and touch someone." Health professionals can have a healing or a magic touch.

Please include much touching during your visit. Hold hands and look your friend in the eye. Be sure to hug each other (in and around the tubes, if necessary). Both casual and intentional massage can offer relaxation and comfort.

Whenever your inner voice says, "I wish I could do something," you can touch your friend.

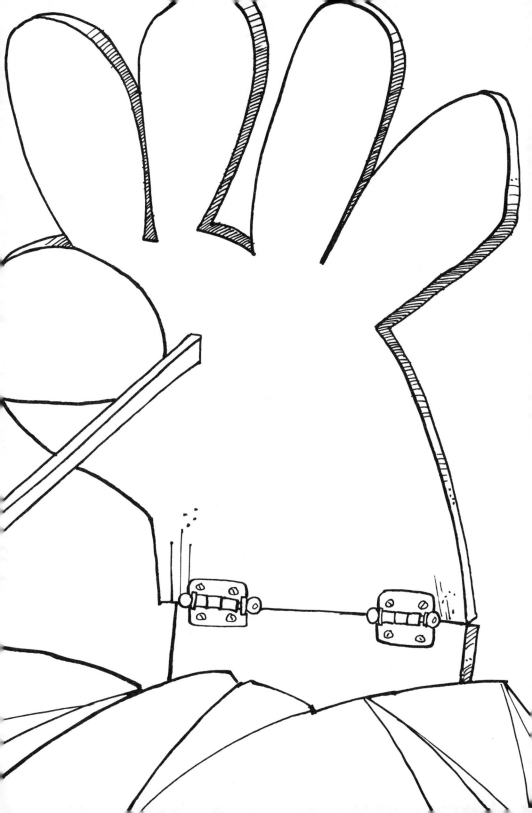

What Can You Do For Them?

Before you make any offers to help the patient or family, know what your limits are. When you know, make offers. Sometimes helping involves feeding pets and watering plants. Or if the children need care, are you available to help occassionally? If a loved one needs a friend, can you be one? If the patient needs help after leaving the hospital, can he or she stay with you? If being poor is the reason the needed care is not given, can you help with a fund-raiser? All of these gestures build community.

Relax and be yourself. Turn off the TV and engage the patient. Tell a few stories, share some gossip, and make it light. It's such a great time to renew and deepen your friendship.

Please acknowledge the other patient(s) in the room. Introduce yourself and try to remember their names. This helps to create a room with companionship (community) for healing.

Even if the patient is very sick or in a coma, be prepared to stay for a while. Hold your friend's hands or stroke them, while reading or telling a story.

Fun, Play, and Laughter

Fun (humor in action) and the accompanying laughter bring great medicine into the hospital room. Studies show that laughter relieves pain, relaxes stress, and stimulates the immune system. For many people, the humor can come through stories of their past or present that show the funny sides of life.

When sitting with a patient, entertain him or her by telling stories and do so with delightful animation. Relax, you don't need to be a comedian or a clown. The idea is to bring a twinkly eye and a smiling spirit. Be your natural self, as if you were dropping by for tea rather than visiting in the hospital. For an extended stay you can help make the visit a delight for both of you. This will help influence the frequency and length of visits.

Do not presume that if the illness is serious you have to remain solemn. I remember a young man who had cancer that killed him in his twenties. He told me how disturbing it was to constantly have people around him treat him as if were already dead. Friends could not see the cancer in perspective enough to treat him as a regular living person. People are always so much bigger than their illness. Hospitals can use a lot more misbehavior.

Faith

When I was a medical student, I remember being in an emergency room and having to pronounce to a family that their son had died as the result of a car accident. In reviewing his chart, I noticed they were Christians. I had been given no tools in my education to help ease suffering other than pills. I knew that pills were no answer in this situation. I decided to suggest that we pray. To this day, I'm amazed at the power that this gesture had in relieving their suffering. Since then I have insisted on understanding the particular faith of my patient. Whenever patients are suffering I like to encourage them to get in touch with their faith.

Even if you do not share a patient's faith, you can draw upon it when visiting and offering comfort. It is amazing how effective drawing on faith can be even if the patient has rarely practiced it. The key is sincerity. Take the patient's hand and pray together. If patients are very ill it can be comforting to read to them from the texts of their faith. In my many visits to nursing homes, I've found it essential and fun to know hymns. Show tunes are good, too.

Listening

So many things may be going on in a patient's mind that a visitor can offer a great service simply by doing conscious listening. Let your friend talk freely. Show a keen interest in everything, without being impatient. You don't have to offer answers or words of wisdom for this to be of terrific value. Help your friend organize his or her thoughts and questions for the health care providers. In a friendly way, ask questions that may have come up for you, either from what you know about your friend or from your natural curiosity. These moments will draw you closer and lay a framework for deeper intimacy in your future. You may even note how you gain a greater understanding of your relationship to your own health. This suggestion strengthens friendship whether one is in the hospital or not.

HOW TO BE A GOOD HOSPITAL PATIENT

1 Try to understand everything that is going on regarding your health. Make a list of questions to ask. If you're shy about asking questions, have a friend ask for you.

2 Pay close attention to everything that is said. If you're on drugs or quite ill, ask that things be written down so someone can help you understand them later.

3 Spend a lot of time looking at yourself and your life. Is this the life you want? What can you do to be healthier? What changes would you like to make? And how can you begin to make them?

4 Feel your own determination to live and to recover. Feel it grow out of your appreciation for life (or the parts of it that you like) and for the passions life has given you.

 5 Allow yourself to be open and vulnerable to all the love and attention of your visitors. Feel their warmth.

 6 Forgive the imperfections of the care delivery system, the doctors and nurses. A climate of mistrust damages everyone.

7 Think of some things that you could do in bed that you are too busy to do in your regular life—such as writing letters, calling up old friends, or pursuing a hobby.

8 Learn to ask for what you need from your health care providers, your co-workers, family members, and friends.

When you become a patient, you do <u>not</u> lose your identity. Be yourself. Hang some art that inspires you. Listen to music that makes you feel good. Bring your own pillow and pillowcase!

Try to be courteous to everyone who works in the hospital. Make sure that your room is a joy for them to enter.

10 When you feel up to it, visit other patients and cheer them up. This is a good opportunity to practice your listening skills.

11 Daydream frequently on things that please you.

12 Plan to come back to the hospital as a volunteer.

SPECIAL CONCERNS WHEN VISITING...

Children

Children are not small adults. A hospital stay can be very scary and much slower than a child's usual life. A lot has been accomplished to make hospitals more fun for children than for adults.

It's a blessing that many hospitals allow a parent to spend the night with the child. Video games and TV have been a big help to pass the time but often a visitor can be frustrated by having to compete with the screen. In a hospital, be content to play in the patient's world. If you know the child, come prepared to play games he or she likes. This is a great time to let your goofy side take charge. When you are funny, it can uplift the rest of the ward and help everyone. Illness can cause a child to become cranky or quiet. Accept kids as they are and show tenderness.

However they act, children appreciate your visit. It helps to divert their fears and loneliness. Sometimes very sick children show grand heroism. Let this inspire you when you tackle problems in your own life.

Teenagers

As in life outside the hospital, teenagers seem to respond best to visits by other teenagers—often the more the merrier. Teenagers can be awkward and hesitant communicators wherever they are. If you normally know how to be with them comfortably, your visit can be a special gem. Listening well and focusing your attention on the patient have healing powers. If you are uncomfortable with teens, your best bet may be to help their peers get transportation to and from the hospital.

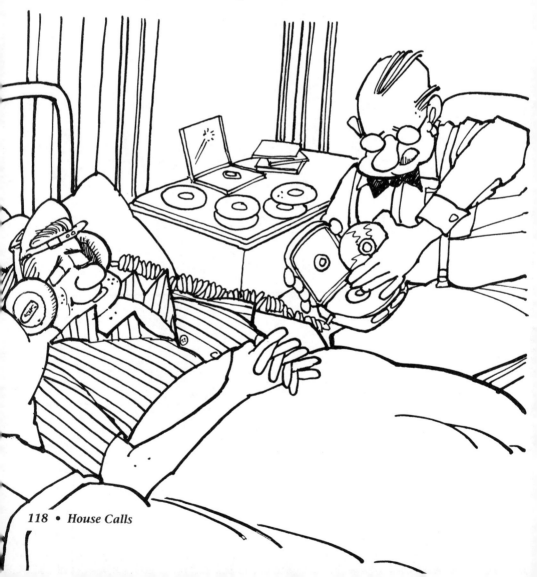

The Elderly

Here, the key is showing up. So much of our elderly population is lonely and disconnected from family and society. Many live unhappy lives in nursing homes. I encourage everyone to visit our elderly, whether in their home, hospital, or nursing home. Stick around, listen to their tales, and catch them up with you and the world. Try not to be in a hurry. Learn to be comfortable in their often shrunken world. Be ready to walk slowly and speak louder. Do not assume that their interests and enthusiasms have waned.

Have the patience to wade through their resignations and feelings of being a burden until you find the sparkle in their eyes. They often feel that people look through them and have put them on the shelf. Be respectful and interested in their history and wisdom. Include them in your outings. If you're looking to feel better about yourself, go regularly to nursing homes and be a companion, going from bed to bed. Touch people, sing to them, and get their blood flowing. You can palpably see them come to life (and the same may happen to you!).

The Mentally Ill

Relax. Everyone is crazy to someone. If you're a people watcher, then a mental hospital or patient can be a grand privilege. Most mentally ill people are not dangerous; rather they have unique ways of thinking and acting. Many are first cousins to eccentrics and they are quite lovable.

So much of what is called "mental illness" is really a consequence of our troubled society—one that promotes loneliness and conformity in a world whose gods are money and power.

During my 30 years in medicine, I have often found that mental patients who are given love, creativity, and community find the peace that they are reaching out for. This can even alter their symptoms.

If your home offers such an environment and you wish to experience the joy of community service, you may consider taking them in. The point is not to be custodial; rather to integrate them into your family, insisting that they help with chores. Ideally, you may find some kind of work that suits their gifts. In this situation, listening skills are especially crucial. Making rational declarations (such as "pull yourself together") may not always be useful. In fact, finding a way to enjoy the pieces may be more appropriate.

The greatest thing each of us can do is to find our own mental health by eliminating boredom, loneliness, and fear in our life. Then we can radiate our mental health publicly as an example of what is possible. Beware of people who think they are "normal."

The Disabled

We most appreciate the value of a body part when we have lost full use of it. In the last half of this century, there has been a dramatic shift toward improving the functioning of disabled persons. Unfortunately, there has also been a shift away from having extended families and communities care for the disabled. This would provide a more favorable environment. It can be dangerous and unhealthy for disabled people to be left alone to care for themselves or to be cared for by just one other person. For the same reason "it takes a whole village to raise a child," a whole village is optimal to provide care for the disabled.

Few things teach patience like the adjustments that must be made in relationships with disabled people. Rather than feeling pity and a sense of burden, use these relationships to celebrate our interdependence. Few things can build true community and a personal sense of security better than the sustained, joyful effort of collectively helping a disabled person day to day.

When you visit a newly disabled person, try to assess what role you can have in helping him or her. Then offer to do what you can. Don't offer anything that you cannot do. The most expensive and lonely systems of care involve hiring strangers or placing people in institutions. Become familiar with all of the organizations in your area, including support groups that are set up to help. Consider pioneering such a group if there are none. Become familiar with the many ingenious devices that can ease the life of a disabled person.

Disabled people want reassurance that they still fill a useful, meaningful role, so help make this a reality. Some of the most inspiring stories in life come from the experiences we have with disabled people who have overcome their challenges.

When you are visiting a disabled person, be as natural as you would be with anyone else. Do not abandon your sense of humor. I have known entire families who have shaved their heads in support of a bald family member enduring cancer treatment. Act out in solidarity!

When a patient is in a coma, assume that they still hear and feel your presence. I encourage visitors to have long conversations with and read to these people—and, of course, touch them a lot. I have been known to put rubber noses on patients who are in a coma to try to lighten up the atmosphere around them.

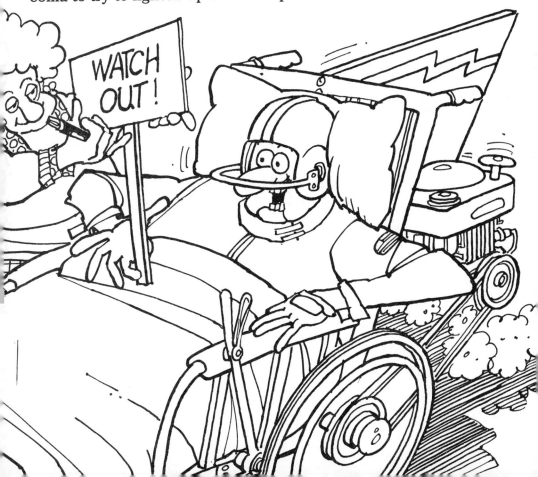

Dying Patients

"Death is not a failure of medical science but the last act of life."
                              – Patch Adams, M.D.

Death can come as a sudden, unexpected horror (as an accident) or a welcome blessing (after a long or painful illness). It is time to bring death back into the fold of a natural community ritual. As natural childbirth has taken away most of the fear of birth and made it a celebration, so too, we can learn to "midwife" death.

Many who are dying or experiencing others dying feel lonely and afraid. When death occurs at home one can feel a strong bond with all involved. This feeling can be experienced in the hospital as well. It is a privilege to be present when a loved one dies. The comfort to the dying is obvious and we get to say "goodbye."

The subject of death in general and our own death should be part of normal conversation to help make it a part of community. One of the most important medical reasons for one to have a strong, active faith is its contribution to comfort and ease around death. If you are visiting someone who is dying, do not look or act as if they are already dead. As long as they are alive, be yourself—if that self is loving, friendly, vivacious, and fun. Can you imagine how discomforting it must be to a dying person to have only gloomy, uncomfortable friends around for the last moments? Let dying people call the shots. If they want quiet and want to sleep, great. It is their time, so don't hold them back. Become familiar with the fine books written on this subject and consider a living will. Also consider the donation of organs if possible. Be respectful of the culture of the person dying and of the family.

Much of the discomfort around death can arise from unfinished business in relationships. Therefore, it behooves us to keep our communication clear at all times. I strongly feel that death is actually a small concern compared to the living dead, who have not fulfilled their dreams or who have not been true to themselves. Live a life for which you can be thankful.

I love this poem by Pablo Neruda for it carries my sentiments:

If I die, survive me with such sheer force
that you waken the furies of the pallid and the cold,
from south to south, lift your indelible eyes,
from sun to sun dream through your singing mouth.
I don't want your laughter or your steps to waver.
I don't want my heritage of joy to die.
Don't call up my person. I am absent.
Live in my absence as if in a house.
Absence is a house so fast
that inside you will pass through its walls
and hang pictures on the air.
Absence is a house so transparent
that I, lifeless, will see you, living,
and if you suffer, my love, I will die again.

BEGINNING

In November 1997, after my annual clown tour to Russia, I took twenty-two clowns to Bosnia. I wanted to bring joy to the worst of situations, war. I had never been so near war before. It felt as if we were making a "house call" on a collective of suffering. I cried a lot and clowned a lot. I came home more committed than ever to try to increase the joy and love among people.

I suggest that whatever you bring to patients to enhance their healing and cheer them up, you can also share with everyone you meet. Each one of us can contribute toward creating a healthier society. It is well documented that helping others benefits one's own health (physically, mentally, and spiritually). And you don't have to give up anything in order to help others.

Things To Do:

1. Get a clown costume (or another costume that makes you feel jovial) and visit nursing home patients. Go from bed to bed— holding their hands, listening, and sharing your passions. Feel this giving you a lift as well.

2. Go by yourself or with a group of friends to serenade people on street corners or in shopping malls. Sing to people who are at work—such as toll booth attendants or grocery clerks.

3. Take a vacation with your family and do volunteer work for Habitat for Humanity or some other service organization.

4. Get a group of friends together and offer to care for children of single parents. You could place an ad in a local paper offering to give both the parent and the child a special day.

The important thing here is to see how good community service makes you feel. I often hear doctors and nurses talk about how the time spent donating their talents at free clinics or on overseas service projects is the most meaningful part of their work. Giving to others is really a gigantic gift to yourself.

Wheee!

BIBLIOGRAPHY

A Booklover's Search for Understanding & Ideas

Welcome to my library! Ever since my high school days, books and magazines have been to my mind what friends are in the flesh. Each and every one of these books and articles—a fraction of the 12,000 volumes that I share my house with—has contributed to expanding my dream.

Dear reader, you have gotten off easy. I have left out the bulk of the philosophy that lives in the world's great fiction, poetry, drama, art, cartoons, and natural sciences, as well as the 120 periodicals that come into our house (among them are the *Food Insect Newsletter*, *Experimental Musical Instruments*, and *Funny Times*).

Use this Bibliography to explore your own questions and ideas about medicine and community: browse, peruse, explore, and dig in! When you come to Gesundheit Institute and seek out the written word, I shall wear the crown of librarian.

Health and Healing

A Free Clinic Starting Out. Roanoke, VA: The Free Clinic Foundation of America, 1992.

Ader, Robert, Nicholas Cohen, and David L. Felten, eds. *Psychoneuroimmunology*, 2nd edition. San Diego: Academic Press, 1991.

Andrews, Charles. *Profit Fever: The Drive to Corporatize Health Care and How to Stop it.* Monroe, Maine: Common Courage Press, 1995.

Balint, Michael, M.D. *The Doctor, His Patient and the Illness.* London: Pitman Medical, 1973.

Bauer, Jefferey. *Not What the Doctor Ordered: Reinventing Medical Care in America.* Chicago: Probus Books, 1994.

Bentley, Joseph D., M.D. *The Betrayal of Health.* New York: Times Books, 1991.

Berger, John. *A Fortunate Man.* New York: Pantheon Books, 1967.

Blanton, Smiley. *Love or Perish.* New York: Simon & Schuster, 1956.

Bogdanich, Wat. *The Great White Lie: Dishonesty, Waste, and Incompetence in the Medical Community.* New York: Simon and Schuster, 1991.

Brown, E. Richard. *Rockefeller Medicine Men.* Berkeley, CA: University of California Press, 1979.

Broyard, Anatsle. *Intoxicated by My Illness and Other Writings on Life and Death.* New York: Clarkson Potter, 1992.

Buchanan, James. *Patient Encounters: The Experience of Disease.* Charlottesville, VA: University of Virginia Press, 1989.

Buckman, Robert, M.D. *How to Break Bad News: A Guide for Health Care Professionals.* Baltimore: The John Hopkins University Press, 1992.

Buscaglia, Leo. *Living, Loving and Learning.* New York: Ballantine Books, 1982.

Caldicott, Helen, M.D. *If You Love this Planet: A Plan to Heal the Earth.* New York: W.W. Norton, 1992.

Califano, Joseph A., Jr. *America's Health Care Revolution.* New York: Simon & Schuster, 1986.

Callahan, Daniel. *What Kind of Life—The Limits of Medical Progress.* New York: Simon & Schuster, 1990.

Callander, Meryn G. and John W. Travis, M.D. *Wellness for Helping Professionals: Creating Compassionate Cultures.* Mill Valley, CA: Wellness Associates Publications, 1990.

Campo, Raphael. *The Poetry of Healing.* New York: W.W. Norton & Co., 1997.

Cassell, Eric J., M.D. *The Healer's Art.* Cambridge, MA: MIT Press, 1986.

———. *The Nature of Suffering.* New York: Oxford University Press, 1991.

———. *Talking With Patients, Vols. 1 and 2.* Cambridge, MA: MIT Press, 1985.

Cassell, Eric J., M.D., and Mark Siegler, M.D. *Changing Values in Medicine.* New York: University Publications of America, Inc., 1979.

Charman, Robert C., M.D. *At Risk: Can the Doctor-Patient Relationship Survive in a High-Tech World?* Dublin, NH: William L. Bauhan, 1992.

Chopra, Deepak, M.D. *Quantum Healing.* New York: Bantam Books, 1989.

Clinebell, Howard, PhD. *Well Being: A Personal Plan for Exploring and Enriching the Seven Dimensions of Life: Mind, Body, Spirit, Love, Work, Play, Earth.* San Francisco: Harper San Francisco, 1992.

Coles, Robert. *The Call of Service: A Witness to Idealism.* New York: Houghton Mifflin, 1993.

Cook, Trevor. *Samuel Hahnemann.* Wellingborough, UK: Thorsons Publishers Ltd., 1981.

Corey, Saltman Epstein. *Medicine in A Changing Society.* St. Louis: C.V. Mosby, 1977.

Coulter, Harris L. *Divided Legacy: The Conflict Between Homeopathy and the American Medical Association, 2nd ed.* Berkeley: North Atlantic Books Homeopathic Educational Services, 1982.

Cousins, Norman. *Anatomy of An Illness.* New York: W. W. Norton & Co., 1979.

———. *Head First: The Biology of Hope.* New York: Dutton, 1989.

———. *The Healing Heart.* New York: W. W. Norton & Co., 1983.

———. *The Physician in Literature.* New York: Saunders Press, 1982.

Csikszentmihalyi, Mihaly. *Flow: The Psychology of Optimal Experience.* New York: Harper & Row, 1990.

Curnen, Mary, Enid Peschell, Howard Spiro, and Deborah St. James, eds. *Empathy and the Practice of Medicine.* New Haven: Yale Univ. Press, 1993.

Dass, Ram, and Paul Gorman. *How Can I Help—Stories and Reflections on Service.* New York: Alfred A. Knopf, 1985.

Donaghue, Paul J., PhD. and Mary E. Siegel, PhD. *Sick and Tired of Feeling Sick and Tired of Feeling Sick...* New York: W.W. Norton & Co., 1992.

Dossey, Larry, M.D. *Be Careful What You Pray For.* San Francisco: Harper San Francisco, 1998.

———. *Prayer Is Good Medicine.* San Francisco: Harper San Francisco, 1997.

———. *Healing Words: The Power of Prayer and the Practice of Medicine.* San Francisco: Harper San Francisco, 1993.

———. *Recovering the Soul: A Scientific and Spiritual Search.* New York: Bantam Books, 1989.

———. *Space, Time and Medicine.* Boston: New Science Library, 1982.

Drane, James F. *Becoming A Good Doctor: The Place of Virtue and Character in Medical Ethics.* Kansas City, MO: Sheed and Ward, 1988.

Dubos, Rene. *Mirage of Health.* New York: Doubleday Anchor Books, 1959.

———. *So Human An Animal.* New York: Charles Scribner, 1968.

Dyson, Burton, M.D., and Elizabeth Dyson. *Neighborhood Caretakers— Stories, Strategies and Tools for Healing Urban Communities.* Indianapolis: Knowledge Systems, 1989.

Dooley, Tom. *Dr. Tom Dooley's Three Great Books.* New York: Farrar, Straus & Cudahy, 1960.

Eliade, Mircea. *Shamanism.* Princeton, N.J.: Princeton Univ. Press, 1964.

Foss, Lawrence, and Kenneth Rothaberg. *The Second Medical Revolution.* Boston: New Science Library, 1987.

Frank, Arthur W. *The Wounded Storyteller: Body, Illness, and Ethics.* Chicago: The University of Chicago Press, 1995.

Frohock, Fred M. *Healing Powers, Alternative Medicine, Spiritual Communities, and the State.* Chicago: The University of Chicago Press, 1992.

Fromm, Erich. *The Art of Loving.* New York: Harper & Row, 1956.

Galen: *Hippocrates. Volume 10, Great Books.* Chicago: Encyclopedia Britannica, 1952.

Geis, Gilbert, Paul Jesilow and Henry N. Pontell. *Prescription for Profit: How Doctors Defraud Medicaid.* Berkeley: University of California Press, 1993.

Gerteis, Margret, and Susan Edgman-Levitan. et. al. *Through the Patient's Eyes.* San Francisco: Jossey-Bass Publishers, 1993.

Goldberg Group, The Burton. *Alternative Medicine: The Definitve Guide.* Tiburon, CA: Future Medicine Publishing, 1994.

Goodnou, John C. and Gerald Musgrave. *Patient Power: Solving America's Health Care Needs.* Washington, D.C.: Cato Institute, 1992.

Gordon, James. *Manifesto for a New Medicine.* Reading, MA: Addison-Wesley Publishing Co., 1996.

Greenberg, Michael, M.D. *Off the Pedestal: Transforming the Business of Medicine.* Houston, TX: Breakthrough Publishing, 1990.

Hammerschlag, Carl A., M.D. *The Dancing Healers: A Doctor's Journey of Healing with Native Americans.* New York: Harper Collins, 1989.

———. *The Theft of the Spirit: A Journey to Spiritual Healing with Native Americans.* New York: Simon and Schuster, 1993.

Hay, Ian. *Money, Medicine, and Malpractice in American Society.* New York: Praeger, 1992.

Hertzler, Arthur. *Horse and Buggy Doctor*. New York: Harper Brothers, 1938.

Hetzel, Richard, M.D., ed. *The New Physician*. Boston: Houghton Mifflin, 1991.

Hilfiker, David. *Not All of Us Are Saints*. New York: Hill and Wang, 1994.

Hirshberg, Caryle and Brendan O'Regan. *Spontaneous Remission: An Annotated Bibliography*. Sausalito: Institute of Noetic Sciences, 1993.

Hunter, Kathryn Montgomery. *Doctor's Stories: The Narrative Structure of Medical Knowledge*. Princeton: Princeton University Press, 1992.

Illich, Ivan. *Medical Nemesis—The Expropriation of Health*. New York: Pantheon, 1976.

Jacobs, Pamela D., M.A. *500 Tips For Coping With Chronic Illness*. San Francisco: Robert D. Reed Publishers, 1997.

Jampolsky, Gerald G., M.D. *Love Is Letting Go of Fear*. New York: Bantam Books, 1970.

Jesdow, Paul, Henry N. Pontell, and Gilbert Geis. *Prescription for Profit: How Doctors Defraud Medicare*. Berkeley: University of California Press, 1993.

Jones, James H. *Bad Blood*. New York: The Free Press, 1981.

Jonsen, Albert R. *The New Medicine and the Old Ethics*. Cambridge, MA: Harvard University Press, 1990.

Justice, Blair, Ph.D. *Who Gets Sick*. Los Angeles: Jeremy Tarcher, Inc., 1988.

Kassler, Jeanne, M.D. *Bitter Medicine: Greed and Chaos in American Health Care*. New York: Birch Lane Press, 1994.

Konner, Melvin. *Medicine at the Crossroads: The Crisis With Health Care*. New York: Pantheon Books, 1993.

Kaysen, Susanna. *Girl, Interrupted*. New York: Vintage Books, 1993.

Kleinman, Arthur, M.D. *The Illness Narratives*. New York: Basic Books, 1988.

Krementz, Jill. *How it Feels to Live with a Physical Disability*. New York: Simon and Schuster, 1992.

Lanctot, Gaylaine. *The Medical Mafia: How to Get Out of It Alive and Take Back Our Health and Wealth*. Morgan, Vermont: Key Inc., 1995.

Lantos, John D. *Do We Still Need Doctors?* New York: Routledge, 1997.

Leebov, Wendy, Ed.D. *Service Excellence: The Customer Relations Strategy for Health Care*. Chicago: American Hospital Association Publishing, Inc., 1988.

Levoy, Gregg. *Callings: Finding and Following an Authentic Life*. New York: Harmony Books, 1997.

Lewer, Nick. *Physicians and the Peace Movement*. London: Frank Cass & Co., Ltd., 1992.

Lifton, Robert Jay. *The Protean Self: Human Resilience in an Age of Fragmentation*. New York: Basic Books, 1993.

Lipp, Martin R., M.D. *Respectful Treatment: The Human Side of Medical Care*. New York: Harper & Row, 1977.

Lowenstein, Jerome, M.D. *The Midnight Meal and other Essays about Doctors, Patients, and Medicine*. New Haven: Yale University Press, 1997.

Lown, Bernard. *The Lost Art of Healing*. Boston: Houghton Mifflin Co., 1996.

Macklin, Ruth. *Enemies of Patients: How Doctors are Losing Their Power...And Patients are Losing Their Rights*. New York: Oxford University Press, 1993.

Marti-Ibanez, Felix, M.D. *The Patient's Progress*. New York: M.D. Publications, 1967.

Massad, Stewart. *Doctors and Other Casualties: Stories of Life and Love Among the Healers*. New York: Warner Books, 1993.

Morone, James A. and Gary S. Belkin, ed. *The Politics of Health Care Reform: Lessons from the Past, Prospects for the Future*. Durham: Duke University Press, 1994.

Matthews, Bonnye L. *Chemical Sensitivity: A Guide to Coping with Hypersensitivity Syndrome, Sick Building Syndrome and Other Environmental Illness*. Jefferson, NC: McFarland and Co., Inc., 1992.

McEwen, James, C. Martini, and H. Wilkins. *Participation in Health*. London: Croom Helm, 1983.

Mendelsohn, Robert S., M.D. *Confessions of a Medical Heretic*. Chicago: Contemporary Books, Inc., 1979.

Moore, Allen H., M.D. *Mustard Plasters and Printer's Ink*. New York: Exposition Press, Inc., 1959.

Morris, David B. *The Culture of Pain*. Berkeley, CA: University of California Press, 1991.

Moss, Ralph W. *The Cancer Industry*. New York: Paragon House, 1989.

Nichols, Joe D., M.D., and James Presley. *Please, Doctor, Do Something*. Old Greenwich, CT: The Devin-Adair Company, 1972.

Nolen, William, M.D. *A Surgeon's Book of Hope*. New York: Coward, McCann & Geoghan, 1980.

Noms, Richard, M.D. *The Musician's Survival Manual: A Guide to Preventing and Treating Injuries to Instrumentalists*. St. Louis: International Conference of Symphony and Opera Musicians, 1993.

Oglesby, Paul. *The Caring Physician: The Life of Dr. Francis W. Peabody*. Boston: The Francis Countway Library of Medicine in Cooperation with The Harvard Medical Alumni Association, 1991.

Osler, Sir William. *A Way of Life and Selected Writings*. New York: Dover Books, 1951.

Pagel, Walter. *Paracelsus—An Introduction To Philosophical Medicine in the Era of the Renaissance, 2nd ed*. Basel: S. Karger, 1982.

Pearse, I. H. *The Quality of Life*. Edinburgh: Scottish Academic Press, 1979.

Peck, M. Scott, M.D. *The Road Less Traveled*. New York: Simon & Schuster, 1978.

Pekkanen, John, M.D. *Doctors Talk About Themselves*. New York: Delacorte Press, 1988.

Podvoll, Edward M., M.D. *The Seduction of Madness*. New York: Harper Collins, 1990.

Polk, Steven R., M.D. *The Medical Students Survival Guide*. Trentland Press, 1992.

Prieto, Jorge, M.D. *Harvest of Hope*. Notre Dame, IN: University of Notre Dame Press, 1989.

Reich, Warren T., ed. *Encyclopedia of Bioethics*. New York: Free Press, 1978.

Reynolds, Richard, M.D., and John Stone, M.D., eds. *On Doctoring*. New York: Simon & Schuster, 1991.

Rosenberg, Charles. *The Care of Strangers—The Rise of America's Hospital System*. New York: Basic Books, 1987.

Rodwin, Mark A. *Medicine, Money and Morals*. New York: Oxford University Press, 1993.

Schweitzer, Albert, M.D. *Albert Schweitzer: An Anthology*. Boston: Beacon Press, 1947.

Selzer, Richard. *Mortal Lessons*. New York: Simon & Schuster, 1974.

———. *Taking the World in for Repairs*. New York: William Morrow & Co., 1986.

Shames, Karilee Halo, R.N., PhD. *The Nightingale Conspiracy: Nursing Comes to Power in the 21st Century*. Staten Island: Power Publications, 1993.

Shapiro, Martin, M.D. *Getting Doctored*. Philadelphia: New Society Publishers, 1987.

Sheehan, Susan. *Is There No Place on Earth for Me?* New York: Random House, 1983.

Sherwin, Susan. *No Longer Patient: Feminist Ethics and Health Care*. Philadelphia: Temple University Press, 1992.

Shorter, Edward. *Doctors and Their Patients*. New Brunswick, NJ: Transaction Publishers, 1991.

Siegel, Bernie S., M.D. *Peace, Love & Healing*. New York: Harper & Row, 1989.

———. *Love, Medicine & Miracles*. New York: Harper & Row, 1986.

Smith, John M., M.D. *Women and Doctors: A Physician's Explosive Account of Women's Medical Treatment—and Mistreatment—in America Today and What You Can do About It*. New York: The Atlantic Monthly Press, 1992.

Sontag, Susan. *Illness as Metaphor*. New York: Random House, 1979.

Starr, Paul. *The Social Transformation of American Medicine*. New York: Basic Books, 1982.

Stevens, Rosemary. *In Sickness and In Wealth*. New York: Basic Books, 1989.

Stratton, Owen Tully. *Medicine Many*. London: Univ. of Oklahoma Press, 1989.

Thomas, Lewis. *The Fragile Species*. New York: Charles Scribner's Sons, 1992.

———. *Late Night Thoughts on Listening to Mahler's Ninth Symphony*. New York: Viking Press, 1983.

———. *The Lives of A Cell*. New York: Bantam Books, 1975.

———. *The Medusa and the Snail*. New York: Viking Press, 1978.

———. *The Youngest Science*. New York: Bantam Books, 1984.

Thomasma, David. *Human Life in the Balance*. Louisville, Ky.: Westminster/ John Knox Press, 1990.

Thompson, John, and Grace Goldin. *The Hospital: A Social and Architectural History*. New Haven, CT: Yale University Press, 1975.

Weil, Andrew, M.D. *Health and Healing*. Boston: Houghton Mifflin Co., 1983.

Weiss, Raymond L., and Charles E. Butterworth. *Ethical Writings of Maimonides*. New York: New York University Press, 1975.

Werner, David, and David Sanders. *The Politics of Primary Health Care and Child Survival*. Palo Alto, CA: Healthwrights, 1997.

Williamson, G. Scott, and Innes H. Pearse. *Science, Synthesis and Sanity*. Edinburgh: Scottish Academic Press, 1980.

Wohl, Stanley, M.D. *The Medical Industrial Complex*. New York: Harmony, 1984.

Wolf, Stewart, and John G. Bruhn. *The Power of Clan: The Influence of Human Relations on Heart Disease*. New Brunswick: Transaction Publishers, 1993.

Physicians' Values

Alda, Alan. "Alan Alda's Prescription for Doctors." *Good Housekeeping.* October 1979.

Barber, Bernard, Ph.D. "Compassion in Medicine: Toward New Definitions and New Institutions." *Seminars in Medicine of Beth Israel Hospital* 295, no. 17 (1976).

Bowen, Otis R., M.D. "Shattuck Lecture—What Is Quality Care?" *New England Journal of Medicine* 316, no. 25 (1987).

Boyle, Joseph F., M.D. "Should We Learn to Say No?" *JAMA* 252, no. 6 (1984).

Bunker, John P. "When Doctors Disagree." *New York Review of Books* April 25, 1985.

Burnum, John, M.D. "Medical Practice a la Mode." *New England Journal of Medicine* 317, no. 19 (1987).

Cassel, Eric J., M.D. "The Nature of Suffering and the Goals of Medicine." *New England Journal of Medicine* 306, no. 11 (1982).

Cohen, Carl I., M.D., and Ellen J. Cohen, Ph.D. "Health Education, Panacea, Pernicious or Pointless." *New England Journal of Medicine* 299, no. 13 (1978).

Coles, Robert, M.D., "The Doctor Is In." *Common Cause Magazine* May/June 1988, pp. 25–29.

Corboy, John, M.D. "Don't Forget the Magic." *American Medical News* June 25—July 2, 1982.

Council of Medical Service. "Quality of Care." *JAMA* 256, no. 8 (1986).

Coury, John Jr., M.D. "Physicians' Fundamental Responsibility." *JAMA* 256, no. 8 (1986).

Darrow, Gregory R., M.D. "If Your Daughter Survives, Doctor, She's Going to be a Gork." *Medical Economics* July 25, 1983.

Deckert, Gordon, M.D. "Urges Physicians to Play More; Avoid Turning Play into Work." *Pediatric News* 20, no. 3 (1986).

Dimsky, S. Edwards, M.D. "Why Not Share the Secrets of Good Health?" *JAMA* 249, no. 23 (1983).

Dirck, John H., M.D. "Sir Thomas Browne (1605–1682)." *JAMA* 248, no. 15 (1982).

Edwards, W. Sterling, M.D. "In Retirement, A Doctor Learns to Truly Listen." *AMA News* October 20, 1989, p. 43.

Gabbard, Glen, M.D. "The Role of Compulsiveness in the Normal Physician." *JAMA* 254, no. 20 (1985).

Guzi, Samuel B., M.D. "Can the Practice of Medicine be Fun for a Lifetime?" *JAMA* 241, no. 19 (1979).

Hilfiker, David, M.D. "Unconscious on a Corner." *JAMA* 258, no. 21 (1987).

Horn, Carole, M.D. "There's Art in Being a Doctor." *Washington Post* October 28, 1984.

Hyman, David. "Fraud and Abuse, Setting Limits on Physicians' Entrepreneurship." *New England Journal of Medicine* 320, no. 19 (1989).

Jansen, Albert R., Ph.D. "Watching the Doctor." *New England Journal of Medicine* 308, no. 25 (1983).

Jirka, Frank J. Jr., M.D. "Travelling New Streets." *JAMA* 250, no. 11 (1983).

John Paul II, Pope. "The Physician and the Rights of Mankind." *JAMA* 251, no. 8 (1984).

Kass, Leon R., M.D., Ph. D. "Ethical Dilemmas in the Care of the Ill." *JAMA* 244, no. 16 (1980).

Korok, Milan. "From Patient Advocate to Gatekeeper." Symposium on Health Care. *American Medical News* April 4, 1986.

Levinson, Wendy, M.D. "Coping with Fallibility." *JAMA* 261, no. 15 (1989).

Marzuk, Peter, M.D. "When the Patient is a Physician." *New England Journal of Medicine* 317, no. 22 (1987).

Mathiasen, Helle, Ph.D., and Joseph Alpert, M.D. "Medicine and Literature in the Medical Curriculum." *JAMA* 244, no. 13 (1980). McClenahan, John L., M.D. "An Apple for the Teacher." *MD* September 1982 p. 13.

McCue, Jack D., M.D. "The Effects of Stress on Physicians and Their Medical Practice." *New England Journal of Medicine* 306, no. 8 (1982).

Nicholson, Ian, "Sometimes, Physicians Need to Take the Time to Care." *AMA News* November 18, 1988, p. 27.

O'Donnell, Walter E., M.D. "Why 'Me First' is Ruining Medicine." *Medical Economics* September 27, 1982.

Osmond, Humphrey, MCRP., F.R.C. Psych., F.R.C.P. "God and the Doctor." *New England Journal of Medicine* 302, no. 10 (1980).

Pellegrino, Edmond, M.D. "Altruism, Self-Interest and Medical Ethics." *JAMA* 258, no. 14 (1987).

Radetsky, Michael, M.D. "Recapturing the Spirit in Medicine." *New England Journal of Medicine* 298, no. 20 (1978).

Risse, Guenter B., M.D. "Whither Healing." *MD*, February 1979.

Rodwin, Marc, M.D. "Physicians' Conflict of Interest." *New England Journal of Medicine* 259, no. 22 (1989).

Southgate, M. Therese, M.D. "Simple Gifts." *JAMA* 245, no. 17 (1981).

Steptoe, Sonja."Dispirited Doctors, Hassles and Red Tape Destroy Joy of the Job for Many Physicians." *Wall Street Journal* April 10, 1987.

Tanay, Emanuel, M.D. "Our Next Endangered Species: The Dedicated Doctor." *Medical Economics* December 7, 1981.

Watts, Malcolm, M.D. "Medicine Has Room for Both 'Breeds' of M.D.s." *AMA News* August 11, 1989, p. 28.

Weed, Lawrence L., M.D. "Physicians of the Future." *New England Journal of Medicine* 304, no. 15 (1981).

Wynen, Andre, M.D. "The World Medical Association and Medical Ethics." *JAMA* 251, no. 8 (1984).

Zinn, William, M.D. "Doctors Have Feelings Too." *New England Journal of Medicine* 259, no. 22 (1988).

Physician Education

Association of American Medical Colleges. "Physicians for the Twenty-First Century." *The GPEP Report*, 1984.

Bickel, Janet. "Human Values Teaching Programs in the Clinical Education of Medical Students." *Journal of Medical Education* May 1987, Vol. 62.

Billings, J. Andrew, M.D., et al. "A Seminar in Plain Doctoring." *Journal of Medical Education* November 1985, Vol. 60.

Brailer, David, M.D. and David Nash, M.D. "Uncertainty and the Future of Young Physicians." *JAMA* 256, no. 24 (1986).

Brauer, Arlette. "Humanizing Medicine." *MD* October 1982.

Bressler, David. "Notes From Overground." *JAMA* 245, no. 16 (1981).

Brown, Sue. "Why New Doctors Aren't Ready for Practice." *Medical Economics* July 25, 1983.

Clark, David, et al. "Vicissitudes of Depressed Mood During Four Years of Medical School." *JAMA* 260, no. 17 (1988).

Cohen, Mark L., M.D. "Uncertainty Rounds." *JAMA* 250, no. 13 (1983).

Colford, John Jr., M.D. "The Ravelled Sleeve of Care, Managing the Stresses of Residency Training." *JAMA* 261, no. 6 (1989).

Council on Long Range Planning and Development of AMA. "Health Care in Transition, Consequences for Young Physicians." *JAMA* 256, no. 24 (1986). "Disaffection of Doctors Is Discouraging Medical Students and Potential Ones." *Wall Street Journal* April 10, 1987.

Dubovsky, Steven L., M.D. and Robert W. Schriu, M.D. "The Mystique of Medical Training." *JAMA* 250, no. 22 (1983).

Eichna, Ludwig W., M.D. "Medical School Education, 1975–1979." *New England Journal of Medicine* 303, no. 13 (1980).

Glick, Seymour M., M.D. "Humanistic Medicine in a Modern Age." *New England Journal of Medicine* 304, no. 17 (1981).

Henry, John Bernard, M.D. "Dean's Welcome Remarks to the Class of 1986." *JAMA* 249, no. 12 (1983).

Johnson, Roger S., Ph.D. "Confront 'Dehumanization' Problem." *Medical Tribune* April 4, 1984.

Kapelman, Loretta, Ph.D. "Cynicism Among Medical Students." *JAMA* 250, no. 15 (1983).

McCue, Jack D., M.D. "The Distress of Internship." *New England Journal of Medicine* 312, no. 7 (1985).

Pence, Gregory E., Ph.D. "Medical Students Need Perspective, Hope." *American Medical News* November 7, 1986.

Perersdorf, Robert G., M.D. "Is the Establishment Defensible." *New England Journal of Medicine* 309, no. 17 (1983).

Rosenberg, Donna A., M.D. and Henry K. Silver, M.D. "Medical Student Abuse." *JAMA* 251, no. 6 (1984).

Schroeder, Steven, M.D. "Academic Medicine as a Public Trust." *JAMA* 262, no. 6 (1989).

Tasteson, D.C., M.D. "Learning in Medicine." *New England Journal of Medicine* September 27, 1979.

Thomas, Lewis. "What Doctors Don't Know." *New York Review of Books* September 24, 1987, p. 6.

Weissmann, Gerald, "A Slap of the Tail: Reading Medical Humanities." *Hospital Practice* June 15, 1988.

Malpractice

Bowen, Otis R., M.D. "Shattuck Lecture—What Is Quality Care?" *New England Journal of Medicine* 316, no. 25 (1987).

Bryan, Charles, M.D. "A M.D. Remembers a Malpractice Suit: 'I've Been There.'" *AMA News* March 17, 1989, p. 55.

Bunker, John P. "When Doctors Disagree." *New York Review of Books* April 25, 1985.

Burnum, John, M.D. "Medical Practice a la Mode." *New England Journal of Medicine* 317, no. 19 (1987).

Challones, David, M.D., et al. "Effects of Liability Crisis on the Academic Health Center." *New England Journal of Medicine* 319, no. 24 (1988).

Cohen, Jon. "Dr. Quixote, Gabor Laufer, M.D., Waged a Private Battle for Tort Reform." *AMA News* March 17, 1989, p. 55.

Council of Medical Service. "Quality of Care." *JAMA* 256, no. 8 (1986).

Coury, John Jr., M.D. "Physicians' Fundamental Responsibility." *JAMA* 256, no. 8 (1986).

Deckert, Gordon, M.D. "Urges Physicians to Play More; Avoid Turning Play into Work." *Pediatric News* 20, no. 3 (1986).

"Fear of Suits Affecting Practice of Medicine." Editorial. *AMA News* June 30, 1989, p. 15.

Gabbard, Glen, M.D. "The Role of Compulsiveness in the Normal Physician." *JAMA* 254, no. 20 (1985).

Goldberg, Joel. "The Great Doctor Revolt." *Medical Economics* July 3, 1989.

Hiatt, Howard, M.D., et al. "A Study of Medical Injury and Medical Malpractice." *New England Journal of Medicine* 321, no. 7 (1989).

Hilfiker, David, M.D. "Unconscious on a Corner." *JAMA* 258, no. 21 (1987).

Horn, Carole, M.D. "There's Art in Being a Doctor." *Washington Post* October 28, 1984.

Korcok, Milan. "From Patient Advocate to Gatekeeper." Symposium on Health Care. *American Medical News* April 4, 1986.

Kubetin, Sally K. "Pediatricians Told To Do More To Confront Crisis in Liability." *Pediatric News* January 1988, p. 2.

Marzuk, Peter, M.D. "When the Patient Is a Physician." *New England Journal of Medicine* 317, no. 22 (1987).

Moskowitz, R., M.D. "Some Thoughts on the Malpractice Crisis." *British Homeopathic Journal* January 1988, p. 77.

Paris, Joseph, M.D. "Current System Will Not Solve Malpractice Crisis." *AMA News* January 8, 1988, p. 40.

Paxton, Harry. "Just How Heavy is the Burden of Malpractice Premiums." *Medical Economy* January 16, 1989.

Pellegrino, Edmond, M.D. "Altruism, Self-Interest and Medical Ethics." *JAMA* 258, no. 14 (1987).

Schwartz, William, M.D., et al. "Physicians Who have Lost Their Malpractice Insurance." *JAMA* 262, no. 10 (1989).

"Special Issue on Malpractice." *Medical Economics* April 18, 1989.

Steptoe, Sonja. "Dispirited Doctors, Hassles and Red Tape Destroy Joy of the Job for Many Physicians." *Wall Street Journal* April 10, 1987.

Doctor-Patient Relationship

Adelson, Bernard H., M.D. "Ethical Decisions in Medicine." *MD* February 1983.

Ansell, David, M.D., and Robert Schiff, M.D. "Patient Dumping." *JAMA* 257, no. 11 (1987).

Cohn, Victor. "Putting the Patients in Charge." *Washington Post* February 26, 1986.

Conger, Charles, M.D. "Now I Know Why Patients Sometimes Scream at Doctors." *Medical Economics* January 16, 1989.

Council on Long Range Planning, AMA House of Delegates. "Survey: M.D.'s Public Image Going Down." *American Medical News* June 28, 1985.

Cousins, Norman. "How Patients Appraise Physicians." *New England Journal of Medicine* 313, no. 22 (1985).

———. "Intangibles in Medicine: An Attempt at Balancing Perspectives." *JAMA* September 23, 1988, p. 26.

———. "The Physician as Communicator." *JAMA* 248, no. 5 (1982).

———. "Unacceptable Pressures on the Physician." *JAMA* 252, no. 3 (1984).

Davidson, Charles, M.D. "Respecting the Autonomy of Competent Patients." *New England Journal of Medicine* 310, no. 17 (1984).

"Deterioration of the Physician/Patient Relationship." Commentary. *American Medical News* October 23, 1987.

Dolan, Barbara, et al. "Doctors and Patients: Image vs. Reality." *TIME* July 31, 1989.

Egeer, Ross L., M.D. "I Make My Patients Be Their Own Doctors." *Medical Economics* June 12, 1978.

Gorlin, Richard, M.D., and Howard D. Zucker, M.D. "Physician's Reaction to Patients." *New England Journal of Medicine* 308, no. 18 (1983).

Hardy, Clyde T. Jr. "What Ever Happened to Dr. Nice Guy." *Medical Economics* February 3, 1986.

Hilfiker, David, M.D. "Facing Our Mistakes." *New England Journal of Medicine* 310, no. 2 (1984).

Hogness, John R., M.D. "What About the Patient?" *New England Journal of Medicine* 313, no. 11 (1985).

Jacoby, M.G., M.B., B.S. "A Father's Letter to a New Intern." *JAMA* 245, no. 10 (1981).

Kassiru, Jerome P., M.D. "Adding Insult to Injury." *New England Journal of Medicine* 308, no. 15 (1983).

Lesser, Gershon, M.D. "Don't Lose Sight of the Human Factor in Patient Care." *AMA News* September 9, 1988, p. 25.

Marzuk, Peter, M.D. "The Right Kind of Paternalism." *New England Journal of Medicine* 313, no. 23 (1985).

Mindell, Benjamin. "Patients Rate Friendliness High Among Physician Traits." *AMA News* February 19, 1988, p. 13.

Neumann, Hans, M.D. "Why Have We Stopped Comforting Patients?" *Medical Economics* June 22, 1987.

Perrone, Janice. "Dr. Davis Urges Physicians: Give a 'Tithe of Your Time'." *AMA News* July 8, 1988, p. 1.

Pinkney, Deborah. "Manpower Crisis." *American Medical News* November 20, 1987.

Quill, Timothy E., M.D. "Patient-Centered Medicine: Increasing Patient Responsibility." *Hospital Practice* November 30, 1985.

Sackler, Arthur M., M.D. "The Doctor Is One of the Patient's Best Friends." *Medical Tribune* June 29, 1983.

Sheldon, Mark, Ph.D. "Truth Telling in Medicine." *JAMA* 247, no. 5 (1982).

Skelly, Flora. "Good M.D.–Patient Relationship Linked to Good Outcome." *AMA News* June 9, 1989, p. 3.

Strull, William M., M.D. et al. "Do Patients Want to Participate in Medical Decision Making?" *JAMA* 292, no. 21 (1984).

Taylor, Flora. "When You and Your Partner The Doctor Talk About Diagnosis." *FDA Consumer* November 1979.

Taylor, Richard, M.D. "Don't Forget Personal in Midst of Technology." *AMA News* May 13, 1988, p. 37.

Teich, Judith. "Primary Care." *JAMA* 259, no. 17 (1988).

Waldron, Vincent D., M.D. "What To Do When Your Patient Isn't Going to Get Better." *Medical Economics* December 20, 1982.

Wassersug, Joseph D., M.D. "What You'll Never Learn Unless You Make House Calls." *Medical Economics* July 22, 1985.

Watts, Malcolm, M.D. "Are Frustrated, Angry M.D.s Good for Health Care?" *AMA News* September 23, 1988, p. 26.

Weaver, James, M.D. "Share Uncertainties of Medical Therapy with Patients." *AMA News* September 9, 1988, p. 32.

Health Care Delivery

"Access to Care and the Evolutions of Corporate, For-Profit Medicine." *New England Journal of Medicine* 311, no. 14 (1984).

Ansell, David, M.D. and Robert Schiff, M.D. "Patient Dumping." *JAMA* 257, no. 11 (1987).

Armitage, Karen J., M.D., et al. "Response of Physicians to Medical Complaints in Men and Women." *JAMA* 241, no. 20 (1979).

Atkins, Charles. "Dollars Must Not Take Precedence Over Care." *AMA News* September 8, 1989, p. 32.

Bezold, Clement. "Health Care in the U.S." *The Futurist* August, 1982.

Bortz , Walter M. II, M.D. "Disuse and Aging." *JAMA* 248, no. 10 (1982).

Califano, Joseph, M.D. "Billions Blown on Health." *New York Times* April 4, 1989.

Castro, Janice. "Critical Condition: Defying All Expectations, Health Costs Continue to Soar." *TIME* February 1,1988, pp. 42–43.

Cohn, Victor. "Caring and Cash Come into Conflict." *Washington Post Health* September 27, 1989, p. 11.

———. "Putting the Patients in Charge." *Washington Post* February 26, 1986.

"Commercialization Said to Threaten M.D.–Patient Trust." Editorial, *Pediatric News* 22, no. 1 (1988).

Couch, Nathan P., M.D., et al. "The High Cost of Low-Frequency Events." *New England Journal of Medicine* 304, no. 11 (1981).

Council on Long Range Planning, AMA House of Delegates. "Survey: M.D.'s Public Image Going Down." *American Medical News* June 28, 1985.

Cousins, Norman. "How Patients Appraise Physicians." *New England Journal of Medicine* 313, no. 22 (1985).

Crawshaw, Ruth, M.D. "Has the Machine Become the Physician?" *JAMA* 250, no. 4 (1983).

Crile, George Jr. "High-Tech Medicine We Can't Afford." *Washington Post* July 31, 1983.

Davis, James E., M.D. "National Initiatives for Care of the Medical Needy." *JAMA* 259, no. 21 (1988).

DeBakey, Michael E., M.D. "Caring Is What Counts." *American Medical News* May 29, 1981.

Del Guercio, Louis R. M., M.D. "Hippocrates Would be Ashamed of Us—Rightfully So!" *Medical Economics* May 15, 1978.

"Deterioration of the Physician/Patient Relationship." Commentary. *American Medical News* October 23, 1987.

Drummond, Hugh, M.D. "Your Health at Too High a Premium." *Mother Jones* May, 1977.

Ehrbar, A.F. "A Radical Prescription for Medical Care." *Fortune* Feb. 1977.

Enthoven, Alain C., Ph.D. "Consumer-Choice Health Plan." *New England Journal of Medicine* 298, no. 12 (1978).

Evans, Robert G. "Controlling Health Expenditures, the Guardian Reality." *New England Journal of Medicine* 320, no. 9 (1989).

Ginzberg, Eli, Ph.D. "The Grand Illusion of Competition in Health Care." *JAMA* 249, no. 10 (1983).

———. "Medical Care for the Poor: No Magic Bullets." *JAMA* 259, no. 21 (1988).

Gould, Jeffrey, M.D. "Socioeconomic Differences with Rate of C-Section." *New England Journal of Medicine* 321, no. 4 (1989).

Goumet, Gerald, M.D. "Health Care Rationing through Rationing." *New England Journal of Medicine* 321, no. 9 (1989).

Gray, James. "How Serious Are Employers About Cutting Health Costs? Very." *Medical Economics* October 16, 1989.

Hancock, Trevor. "Beyond Health Care." *The Futurist* August 1982.

Hardy, Clyde T. Jr. "What Ever Happened to Dr. Nice Guy?" *Medical Economics* February 3, 1986.

"Health Cost: What Limit?" *TIME* May 28, 1979.

Hellman, Alan, M.D., et. al. "How Do Financial Incentives Affect Physician's Clinical Decisions and the Financial Performance of Health Maintenance Organizations?" *New England Journal of Medicine* 321, no. 2 (1989).

Hogness, John R., M.D. "What About the Patient?" *New England Journal of Medicine* 313, no. 11 (1985).

Iglehart, John K., "Payment of Physicians Under Medicare." *New England Journal of Medicine* 318, no. 13 (1988).

———. "The Debate over Physician Ownership of Health Care Facilities." *New England Journal of Medicine* 321, no. 3 (1989).

Kassirer, Jerome, M.D. "Our Stubborn Quest for Diagnostic Certainty." *New England Journal of Medicine* 320, no. 22 (1989).

Kimball, Merit. "AMA Goes to War Against Limits on Doctor Payments." *Health Week* July 17, 1989, p. 9.

———. "Doctors Who Own Labs Order More Costly Tests." *Health Week* June 12, 1989, p.6.

Kinzer, David. "The Decline and Fall of Deregulation." *New England Journal of Medicine* 318, no. 2 (1988).

Kirchner, Merian. "How Much Trouble Is your Hospital in?" *Medical Economics*, December 19, 1988.

Leaf, Alexander, M.D. "Cost Effectiveness as a Criterion for Medicare Coverage." *New England Journal of Medicine* 321, no. 13 (1989).

Linzer, Mark, M.D. "Doing What 'Needs' to Be Done." *New England Journal of Medicine* 310, no. 7 (1984).

Madison, Donald L., M.D. "The Case for Community-Oriented Primary Care." *JAMA* 249, no. 10 (1983).

Marzuk, Peter, M.D. "The Right Kind of Paternalism." *New England Journal of Medicine* 313, no. 23 (1985).

McClenohan, John L., M.D. "On Going to the Doctor." *MD* September 1980.

Morreim, E. Haavi. "Conflicts of Interest—Profits and Problems in Physician Referrals," *JAMA* 262, no. 3 (1989).

Moxley, John III, M.D. "Is the Care of the Chronically Ill a Medical Prerogative?" *New England Journal of Medicine* 310, no. 3 (1984).

Neumann, Hans, M.D. "Why Have We Stopped Comforting Patients?" *Medical Economics* June 22, 1987.

Nowak, Barbara W. "Marketing Medicine to Today's Consumer." *JAMA* 242, no. 22 (1979).

Nuzzo, Roy, M.D. "Medicaid Inequities." Infectious Diseases of Children June 1989, p. 3. Pinkney, Deborah S., "Hospitals Closures Up! Few MDS Patients." *AMA News* May 19, 1989, p. 1.

———. "Manpower Crisis." *American Medical News* November 20, 1987.

———. "Patient's Access to Hospital Care Eroding." *AMA News* February 19, 1988, p. 11.

Plumeri, Peter P., DO, JD, LLM. "Finally . . . A Treatable Illness." *JAMA* 250, no. 10 (1983).

Quill, Timothy E., M.D. "Patient-Centered Medicine: Increasing Patient Responsibility." *Hospital Practice* November 30, 1985.

Reagan, Michael. "Health Care Rationing." *New England Journal of Medicine* 319, no. 12 (1988).

Relman, Arnold, M.D. "The National Leadership Commission's Health Care Plan." *New England Journal of Medicine* 320, no. 5 (1989).

———. "Salaried Physicians and Economic Incentives." *New England Journal of Medicine* 319, p. 12 (1988).

Saltzman, Robert L., M.D. "Time to Return to Basics." *American Medical News* September 28, 1984.

Samuelson, Robert J. "Why Medical Costs Keep Soaring." *Washington Post* November 30, 1988, p. A23.

Saward, Ernest, M.D. "Competition and Health Care." *New England Journal of Medicine* 306, no. 15 (1982).

———. "Reflections on Change in Medical Practice." *JAMA* 250, no. 20 (1983).

Scheier, Ronni. "Learning to Practice the Business of Medicine." *AMA News* January 20, 1989 p. 41.

Schneider, Edward, M.D. "Options to Control the Rising Health Care Costs of Older Americans." *JAMA* 261, no. 6 (1989).

Schramn, Carl J., Ph.D. "Can We Solve the Hospital-Cost Problem in Our Democracy?" *New England Journal of Medicine* 311, no. 11 (1984).

Scoltoch, John, M.D. "Look What the Profit Motive Is Doing to Us Doctors!" *Medical Economics* February 6, 1978.

Siegel, Mark, M.D. "A Physician's Perspective on a Right to Health Care." *JAMA* 244, no. 14 (1980).

Snyder, Richard D. "Health Hazard Appraisal." *The Futurist* August 1982.

Steel, Knight, M.D., et al. "Iatrogenic Illness on a General Medical Service at a University Hospital." *New England Journal of Medicine* 304, no. 11 (1981) .

Strull, William M., M.D., et al. "Do Patients Want to Participate in Medical Decision Making?" *JAMA* 292, no. 21 (1984).

Todd, James S., M.D. "It Is Time for Universal Access, Not Universal Insurance." *New England Journal of Medicine* 321, no. 1 (1989).

Trunet, Patrick, M.D. "The Role of Iatrogenic Disease in Admissions to Intensive Care." *JAMA* 244, no. 23 (1980).

Walsh, H. Gilbert, M.D., et al. "Dealing with Limited Resources." *New England Journal of Medicine* 310, no. 3 (1988).

Wassersug, Joseph D., M.D. "What You'll Never Learn Unless You Make House Calls." *Medical Economics* July 22, 1985.

Watts, Malcolm, M.D. "The Dilemma of Favoring Dollars over Doctoring." *AMA News* November 18, 1988, p. 25.

———. "We're Missing the Point in Cutting Health Costs." *AMA News* 319, p. 27 (1988).

Woolhandler, Steffie, M.D., et al. "A National Health Program: Northern Light at the End of the Tunnel." *JAMA* 262, no. 15 (1989).

Perspectives on Health and Healing

Barsky, Arthur. "The Paradox of Health." *New England Journal of Medicine* 318, no. 7 (1988).

Berwick, Donald, M.D. "Continuous Improvement as An Ideal in Health Care." *New England Journal of Medicine* 320, no. 1 (1989).

Boisaubin, Eugene V., M.D. "A Barefoot Physician." *JAMA* 249, no. 1 (1983).

Close, William, M.D. "Real Medicine, As Practiced in the 'Boonies.' " *AMA News* September 9, 1988, p. 48.

Cranshaw, Ralph, M.D. "A Lesson from Chinese Medicine." *JAMA* November 17, 1978.

Donabedian, Avedis, M.D. "The Quality of Care—How Can It Be Assessed?" *JAMA* 260, no. 12 (1988).

French, Kimberly. "Health-Politics Connection Exposed in New York." *Whole Life Times* January/February, 1983.

Gillick, Muriel B., M.D. "Common-Sense Models of Health and Disease." 313, no. 11 (1985).

Godden, J.O., M.D. "The Role of Belief in the Healing Process." Conference on Continuing Education, McMaster University Medical School. Feb. 3, 1983.

Gorden, James S., M.D. "Holistic Medicine: Toward a New Medical Model." *Journal of Clinical Psychiatry* 42 vol. 3 (1981).

Harris, T. George. "Beyond Self." *American Health* March 1988, pp. 51–71.

Iotta, Dennis, M.D. "Wellness Put My Practice in Shape." *Medical Economics* 220, no. 13 (1988).

Martin, Morgan, M.D. "Native American Medicine." *JAMA* 245, no. 2 (1981).

Meyer, Harris. "Dr. Nelson Urges M.D.s to Stress Humanism." *AMA News* July 1989.

Muna, Walinjam F.T., M.D. "How I Encountered the Sophisticated Traditional Healer." *JAMA* 246, no. 22 (1981).

Nelson, Alan, M.D. "Humanism and the Art of Medicine, Our Commitment to Care." *JAMA* 262, no. 9 (1989).

Pedoisky, M. Lawrence, M.D. "Is Holistic Medicine Filling a Gap We've Created?" *Medical Economics* December 11, 1978.

"Psychiatric Sanctuary." *MD* July 1979.

Seliger, Susan. "Stop Killing Yourself." *Washingtonian* September 1978.

Shapiro, Edith, M.D. "Medical Profession Needs to Regain Its Good Manners." *AMA News*, August 18, 1989, p. 31.

Skelly, Flora. "Beyond Conventional Therapy." *AMA News* November 17, 1989, p. 37.

Steffen, Grant, M.D. "Quality Medical Care." *JAMA* 260, no. 1 (1988).

Wanzer, Sidney, M.D., et al. "The Physician's Responsibility Toward Hopelessly Ill Patients." *New England Journal of Medicine* March 30, 1989.

Watts, Malcolm, M.D. "M.D.s Have Responsibility to Cure Society's Ills." *AMA News*, Jan. 13, 1989, p. 28.

Creativity

Collier, Lindsay. *Get Out Of Your Thinking Box: 365 ways to brighten your life & enhance your creativity*. San Francisco: Robert D. Reed Publishers, 1994.

Gardner, Howard. *Creating Minds*. New York: Basic Books, 1993.

May, Rollo. *The Courage To Create*. New York: Bantam Books, 1975.

Michalko, Michael. *Thinkertoys: A Handbook of Business Creativity*. Berkeley: Ten Speed Press, 1991.

Von Oech, Roger. *A Kick In the Seat of the Pants*. New York: Warner Books, 1986.

_____. *A Whack On the Side of the Head*. New York, Warner Books, 1983.

_____. "How You Can Be More Creative" (Audio tapes) Nightingale-Conant Corporation, 7300 N. Lehigh Avenue, Chicago, IL 60648.

Weber, Robert J. Forks. *Phonographs and Hot Air Balloons, A Field Guide to Inventive Thinking*. New York: Oxford University Press, 1992.

Complementary Medicine

Fugh-Berman, M.D., Adriane. *Alternative Medicine: What Works*. Tucson: Odonian Press, 1996.

Goldberg Group, The Burton. *Alternative Medicine Guide.* Tiburon, CA: Future Medicine Publishing, 1993.

Gordon, M.D., James. *Manifesto For a New Medicine.* Reading, MA: Addison-Wesley Publishing, 1996.

Weil, M.D., Andrew. *Spontaneous Healing.* New York: Alfred A. Knopf, 1995.

Cancer

Cowden, W. Lee, M.D., John Diamond, M.D., with Burton Goldberg. *Burton Goldberg Presents... Alternative Medicine Guide To Cancer.* Tiburon: Future Medicine Publishing, 1997.

Lerner, Michael. *Choices In Healing.* Cambridge, MA: MIT Press, 1994.

Elderly

Covel, Mara. *The Home Alternative To Hospital and Nursing Homes.* New York: An Owl Book, 1983.

Doress, Paula B., et al. *Ourselves, Growing Older.* New York: Touchstone Book, 1987.

Fisher, Pauline. *More Than Movement For Fit To Frail Older Adults.* Baltimore: Health Professions Press, 1995.

Matthews, Joseph. *Elder Care.* Berkeley: Nolo Press, 1990.

The Disabled

Gillett, Dexter. *Tools for Empowerment.* Box 174, Fon-du-Lac, WI 54936.

Griffen, Moira. *Going The Distance: Living A Full Life with Multiple Sclerosis and Other Debilitating Diseases.* New York: Dutton, 1989.

Hale, Glorya, ed. *The Sourcebook For the Disabled.* New York: Paddington Press, 1979.

Kane, M.D., Jeff. *Be Sick Well.* Oakland: New Harbinger, 1991.

Krementz, Jill. *How It Feels To Live With a Physical Disability.* New York: Simon & Schuster, 1992.

Kut, Howard. *Yoga For The Disabled.* New York: Thorsons Publishing, 1986.

Stone, Karen G. *Awakening To Disability.* Volcano, CA: Volcano Press, 1997.

Torch, Deborah. *The Musician's Survival Guide.* San Antonia: Crummue Press, 1993.

Ufchez, Raymond & Barbara Winslow. *Design for Independent Living.* Berkeley: University of California Press, 1979.

Werner, David. *Nothing About Us Without Us Developing Innovative Technologies For, By & With Disabled Persons.* Palo Alto: Healthwrights, 1998.

Products for the Disabled

Able Wear 1-800-443-4926

Adaptability 1-800-243-9232

Handiaid
2907 W. Warner Ave.
Santa Ana, CA 92704

Natl. Library Service For the Blind & Physically Handicapped
The Library of Congress
Washington, D.C. 20542
North Coast Medical 1-800-235-7054

Mental Health

Cohen, Alan. *I Had It All The Time.* Makawao, HI: Alan Cohen Publications, 1995.

Dorris, Michael. *The Broken Cord.* New York: Harper Perennial, 1989.

Farber, Seth. *Madness, Heresy and The Rumor of the Angels.* Chicago: Open Court, 1993.

Hammerschlag, M.D., Carl. "Living With Joy" (Tapes). 3104 East Camelback Road, Suite 614, Phoenix, AZ 85106.

Kaysen, Susanna. *Girl, Interrupted.* New York: Vintage Books, 1993.

May, Rollo. *Man's Search For Himself.* New York: Signet Books, 1953.

Miller, Alice. *The Drama of the Gifted Child.* New York: Basic Books, 1997.

Pepper, John. *How To Be Happy.* London: Arkana, 1985.

Prather, Hugh. *Notes On How To Live In the World...And Still Be Happy.* Garden City, NY: Doubleday & Co., 1986.

Rosen, M.D., David. *Transforming Depression.* New York: Jeremy Tarcher, 1993.

Russell, Bertrand. *The Conquest of Happiness.* Garden City, NY: Garden City Publishing, 1930.

Sheehan, Susan. *Is There No Place On Earth For Me?* New York: Vintage Books, 1982.

Siebert, Al. *Peeking Out My Mind Broke Free From The Delusions In Psychiatry.* Portlant, OR: Practical Psychology Press, 1995.

Siegal, Bryna. *The World of the Autistic Child.* New York: Oxford University Press, 1996.

Suarez, Rick et al. *Sanity, Insanity and Common Sense—A Groundbreaking Approach To Happiness.* New York: Fawcett Columbine, 1987.

Watts, Alan. *The Meaning of Happiness.* New York: Perennial Library, 1940.

Williams, Donna. *Nobody Nowhere, Autobiography of an Autistic.* New York: Times Books, 1992.

Nutrition

Ballentine, M.D., Rudolph. *Diet and Nutrition.* Homesdale, PA: The Himalayan International Institute, 1978.

Haas, Elson. *Staying Healthy With Nutrition.* Berkeley, Celestial Arts, 1992.

Hamilton, Kirk. *Clinical Pearls.* Each year compiles all abstracts from research that year in nutrition. I.T. Services, 3301 Alta Arden #3, Sacramento, CA 95825.

Ornish, M.D., Dean. *Eat More, Weigh Less.* New York: Harper Collins, 1993.

_____, *Stress, Diet and Your Heart.* New York: Holt, Rinehart & Winston, 1982.

Williams, Roger. *Nutrition Against Disease.* New York: Pitman Publishing, 1971.

Play/Clowning

Blatner, M.D., Adam. *The Art of Play*. New York: Human Sciences Press, 1988.

Fluegelman, Andrew. *More New Games*. New York: Dolphin Books, 1981.

_____. *The New Games Book*. New York: Dolphin Books, 1976.

Izzo, Gary. *The Art of Play*. Portsmouth, NH: Heinemann, 1997.

Martin, Joseph F. *Foolish Wisdom*. San Jose: Resource Publ., 1990.

McCullagh, James C. *Ways To Play*. Emmaus, PA: Rodale Press, 1978.

McVior, Wes. *Clown Act Omnibus*. Colorado Springs: Meriweather Publ., 1987.

Nachmanovitch, Stephen. *Freeplay*. Los Angeles: Jeremy Tarcher, 1990.

Pipkin, Turk. *Be A Clown*. New York: Workman Publ., 1989.

Weinstein, Matt and Joel Goodman. *Playfair*. San Luis Obispo: Impact, 1980.

Love

Ackerman, Diane. *The Book of Love*. New York: W. W. Norton, 1998.

Borysenko, Joan. *Guilt Is The Teacher, Love Is The Lesson*. New Yorker: Warner Books, 1990.

Buscaglia, Leo. *Living, Loving & Learning*. New York: Ballantine Books, 1982.

Fromm, Erich. *The Art of Loving*. New York: Bantam Books, 1963.

Jampolsky, M.D., Gerald. *Loving Is Letting Go Of Fear*. New York: Bantam Books, 1979.

May, Rollo. *Love and Will*. New York: W. W. Norton, 1969.

The Mind-Body Connection

Justice, Blair, Ph.D. *Who Gets Sick*. Los Angeles: Tarcher, St. Martin's Press, 1988.

Cousins, Norman. *Head First: The Biology of Hope*. New York: Dutton, 1989.

Ader, Robert, David L. Felten, Nicholas Cohen, eds. *Psychoneuroimmunology*. New York: Academic Press, 1990.

Clinebell, Howard, Ph.D. *Well Being: A Personal Plan For Exploring and Enriching The Seven Dimensions of Life*. San Francisco: Harper San Francisco, 1992.

Eliot, Robert S., M.D. *From Stress To Strength: How To Lighten Your Load and Save Your Life*. New York: Bantam, 1994.

Dacher, Elliott S., M.D. *Whole Healing: A Step-By-Step Program to Reclaim Your Power To Heal*. New York: Dutton, 1996.

Faelten, Sharon, David Diamond and Editors of Prevention Magazine. *Take Control Of Your Life: A Complete Guide To Stress Relief*. Emmaus, PA: Rodale Press, 1988.

Gawler, Ian. *The Mind Body Connection*. The Gawler Foundation: Victoria, Australia, 1996.

Gordon, James S., M.D. *Manifesto for a New Medicine*. Reading, MA: Addison-Wesley Publishing, 1996.

Moyers, Bill. *Healing and The Mind*. New York: Doubleday, 1993.

Rossman, Martin L., M.D. *Healing Yourself*. New York: Pocket Books, 1987.

Stoll, Walt. *Saving Yourself From The Disease Care Crisis*. Panama City, FL: Sunshine Health Coach, 1996.

Weil, Andrew W. *Spontaneous Healing*. New York: Alfred A. Knopf, 1995.

The Joy of Service

Cassell, Eric J. *The Healer's Art*. Cambridge, Massachusetts: MIT Press, 1985.

_____. *The Nature of Suffering and The Goals of Medicine*. New York: Oxford University Press, 1991.

_____. *Talking With Patients, Vol. I: The Theory of Doctor-Patient Communication*. Cambridge, Massachusetts: The MIT Press, 1985.

_____, *Talking With Patients, Vol. II: Clinical Technique*. Cambridge, MA: The MIT Press, 1985.

Coles, Robert. *The Call of Service: A Witness to Idealism*. Boston: Houghton Mifflin Company, 1993.

Dass, Ram and Mirabai Bush. *Compassion In Action: Setting Out on the Path of Service*. New York: Bell Tower, 1992.

Dass, Ram and Paul Gorman. *How Can I Help?* New York: Alfred A. Knopf, 1994.

Gerteis, Margaret; Susan Edgman-Levitan, Jennifer Daley, and Thomas L. Delbanco, eds. *Through the Patient's Eyes*. San Francisco: Jossey-Bass, 1993.

Kleinman, Arthur, M.D. *The Illness Narratives*. New York: Basic Books, 1988.

Oglesby, Paul, M.D. *The Caring Physician: The Life of Dr. Francis W. Peabody*. Boston: The Francis A. Countway Library of Medicine, 1991.

Reynolds, Richard, M.D., and John Stone, M.D. *On Doctoring*. New York: Simon & Schuster, 1991.

Roter, Debra L. and Judith A. Hall. *Doctors Talking with Patients/Patients Talking with Doctors*. Westport, CT: Auburn House, 1992.

Humor and Health

Baudelaire, Charles. "The Essence of Laughter," in Essays. New York: Meridian Books, 1956.

Berger, Peter L. *Redeeming Laughter*. New York: Walter de Gruyter & Co., 1997.

Bergson, H. Laughter. *An Essay on the Meaning of the Comic*. New York: Macmillan, 1911.

Berk, Lee S., et. al. "Neuroendocrine and Stress Hormone Changes During Mirthful Laughter." *The American Journal of the Medical Sciences*, Vol. 296, No. 7, December 1989.

Beyondananda, Swami. *When You See a Sacred Cow...Milk It For All It's Worth*. Lower Lake, CA: Aslan Publishing, 1993.

Blair, W. "What's Funny About Doctors." *Perspectives in Biology and Medicine*, 1977.

Blumenfeld, E., and L. Alpern. *The Smile Connection*. Englewood Cliffs, NJ: Prentice Hall, 1986.

Bokun, Branko. *Humour Therapy*. London: Vita Books, 1986.

Boston, R. *An Anatomy of Laughter*. London: Collins, 1974.

Boxman, Karyn, RN. "Humor in Therapy for the Mentally Ill." *Journal of Psychosocial Nursing*, Vol. 29, No. 12, 1991.

Burton, Robert. *The Anatomy of Melancholy*. New York: Tudor Publishing, 1927.

Chapman, A. J., and H. C. Foot. eds. *It's A Funny Thing, Humor*. International Conference on Humor and Laughter. Oxford: Pergamon Press, 1976.

Coser, R. L. "Some Social Functions of Laughter: A Study of Humor in a Hospital Setting." *Human Relations*, 1959.

Cousins, Norman. *Anatomy of An Illness*. New York: W. W. Norton, 1979.

Dana, Bill, and Laurence, Peter. *The Laughter Prescription*. New York: Ballantine, 1982.

Dearborn, G. V. N. "The Nature of the Smile and the Laugh." *Science*, 1900.

Euck, John J., Elizabeth Forter, Alvin Whitley, eds. *The Comic in Theory and Practice*. New York: Appleton-Century-Crofts, 1960.

Fairbanks, Douglas. *Laugh and Live*. New York: Britton Publishing, 1917.

Feibleman, James. *In Praise of Comedy*. New York: Horizon Press, 1970.

Freud, Sigmund. *Jokes and Their Relationship to the Unconscious*. New York: W.W. Norton & Co., 1964.

Fry, W. F., Jr., *Sweet Madness: A Study of Humor*. Palo Alto, CA: Pacific, 1963.

____. *Make 'Em Laugh*. Palo Alto: Science & Behavior, 1975.

____ and C. Rader. "The Respiratory Components of Mirthful Laughter." *Journal of Biological Psychology*, 1977.

____ and Waleed A. Salameh PhD., eds. *Advances in Humor and Psychology*. Sarasota: Professional Resource Press, 1993.

Gaberson, Kathleen B., RN. "The Effect of Humorous Disfunction on Preoperative Anxiety." *AORN Journal*, Vol. 54, No. 6, December 1991.

Glodstein, Jefferey H. and Paul McGhee, eds. *Handbook of Humor Research*. Basic Issues Vol. 1; Applied Studies Vol. 2. New York: Springer-Verlag, 1983.

Goodheart, Annette. *Laughter Therapy*. Santa Barbara: Less Stress Press, 1994.

Grotjahn, M. *Beyond Laughter*. New York: McGraw-Hill, 1956.

Hageseth, Christian, III, M.D. *A Laughing Place*. Ft. Collins, CO: Berwick Publishing, 1988.

Haller, Bernard and Rita Zarai. *Rire c'est la Santé*. Geneva: Éditions Soleil, 1986.

Harlow, H. F. "The Anatomy of Humor." *Impact of Science on Society*, 1969.

Hassett, J., and G. E. Schwartz. "Why Can't People Take Humor Seriously?" *New York Times Magazine*, February, 1977.

"The Healing Power of Laughter and Play: Uses of Humor in the Healing Arts." (Twelve tapes) P.O. Box 94305, Portola Valley, CA: IAHB, Inc., 1983.

Holden, Robert. *Laughter the Best Medicine*. London: Thorsons, 1993.

Holland, Norman. *Laughing: The Psychology of Humor*. New York: Cornell University Press, 1982.

Hyde, Lewis. *Trickster Makes the World*. New York: Farrar, Straus & Giroux, 1998.

Joubert, Laurent. *Treatise on Laughter*. Birmingham, AL: University of Alabama Press, 1970.

Keller, Dan. *Humor as Therapy*. Wau Watosh, WI: Med-Psych Publ., 1984.

Klein, Allen. *The Healing Power of Humor*. Los Angeles: Jeremy Tarcher, 1989.

Koestler, A. *The Act of Creation*. New York: Macmillan, 1964.

Levine, J. "Humor as a Form of Therapy" in *It's A Funny Thing, Humor*, ed. by A. J. Chapman and H. C. Foot. Oxford: Pergamon Press, 1976.

McConnell, J. "Confessions of a Scientific Humorist." *Impact of Science on Society*, 1969.

McHale, Maryellen, RN. "Getting the Joke: Interpreting Humor in Group Therapy." *Journal of Psychological Nursing*, Vol. 27, No. 9, 1989.

Metcalf, C.W. and Roma Felible. *Lighten Up*. Reading, MA: Addison-Wesley Publishing Co., 1992.

Mind, H. "The Use and Abuse of Humor in Psychotherapy" in *Humor and Laughter: Theory, Research and Application*, ed. by A. J. Chapman and H. C. Foot. New York: John Wiley & Sons, 1976.

Mindess, Harvey, et al., eds. *The Antioch Humor Test*. New York: Avon, 1985.

——. "Laughter and Humor in Medical Practice." *Behavioral Medicine*, 1979.

Moody, R. A., Jr. *Laugh After Laugh: The Healing Power of Humor*. Jacksonville, Fl.: Headwaters Press, 1978.

Paskind, H. A. "Effect of Laughter on Muscle Tone." *Archives of Neurology and Psychiatry*, 1932.

Pasquali, Elaine Anne, PhD. "Learning to Laugh: Humor as Therapy." *Journal of Psychological Nursing*, Vol. 28, No. 3, 1990.

Pirandello, Luigi. *On Humor*. Chapel Hill, N.C.: University of North Carolina Press, 1974.

Potter, Stephen. *The Sense of Humor*. Middlesex, England: Penguin, 1954.

Robinson, Vera. *Humor and Health*. In J. H. Goldstein and P. McGhee, eds. Handbook of Humor Research. New York: Springer-Verlag, 1983.

____. *Humor and the Health Professions*. Throfare, NJ: Slack Co., 1977.

Samra, Cal. *The Joyful Chant: The Healing Power of Humor*. San Francisco: Harper & Row, 1986.

____. *Holy Humor*. New York: Master Media Ltd., 1996.

Sanders, Barry. *Sudden Glory—Laughter As Subversive History*. Boston: Beacon Press, 1995.

Schachter, S., and L. Wheeler. "Epinephrine, Chlorpromazine, and Amusement." *Journal of Abnormal and Social Psychology*, 1962.

Schaller, Christian Tal. *Rire Pour Gai-Rire*. Geneva, Éditions Vivez Soleil, 1994.

Spenser, H. "The Physiology of Laughter." *Macmillan's Magazine*, 1860.

Vergeer, Gwen and Anne MacRae. "Therapeutic Use of Humor in Occupational Therapy." *American Journal of Occupational Therapy*, Vol. 47, No. 8, Aug. 1993.

Wooten, Patty, ed. *Heart Humor and Healing*. Mount Shasta, CA: Commune-A-Key Publishing, 1994.

Zillmann, Dolf, et. al. "Does Humor Facilitate Coping with Physical Discomfort?" *Motivation and Emotion*, Vol. 17, No. 1, 1993.

____, et. al. "Eustress of Mirthful Laughter Modifies Natural Killer Cell Activity." *Clinical Research*, Vol. 37, No. 1, January 1989.

____, et. al. "Modulation of Human Natural Killer Cells by Catecholamines." *Clinical Research*, Vol. 32, No. 1, November 1984.

____ and eds. *Handbook of Humor and Psychology*. Sarsota: Professional Resources Press, 1987.

Death and Pain
Personal Accounts
Alexander, Victoria. *Words I Never Thought to Speak: Stories of Life in the Wake of Suicide*. New York: Lexington Books, Imprint of Macmillan, 1991.

Baier, Sue, and Mary Zimmeth. *Bed Number Ten*. New York: Holt, 1985.

Beauvoir, Simone de. *A Very Easy Death*. New York: Pantheon Books, 1965.

Brodley, Harold. *This Wild Darkness*. New York: Henry Holt & Co., 1996.

Broyard, Anatole. *Intoxicated By My Illness and Other Writings on Life & Death*. New York: Clarkson/Potter Publisher, 1992.

Byock, M.D., Ira. *Dying Well*. New York: Riverhead Books, 1997.

Gunther, John. *Death Be Not Proud*. New York: Harper & Row, 1949.

Humphrey, Derek. *Jean's Way*. Los Angeles: The Hemlock Society, 1984.

———. *Let Me Die Before I Wake*. Los Angeles: The Hemlock Society, 1981.

Huxley, Laura. *The Timeless Moment*. Berkeley, CA: Celestial Arts, 1975.

"Prevention Magazine" eds. *Pain-Relief System*. Emmasu, PA: Rodale, 1992.

Lang, Susan and Richard Patt. *You Don't Have To Suffer*. New York: Oxford Crown Press, 1994.

Middlebrook, Christina. *Seeing The Crab: A Memoir of Dying*. New York: Anchor Books, 1996.

Robinson, Jess. *The Best We Could Do*. Published by author, 1982.

Rollin, Betty. *Last Wish*. New York: Simon & Schuster, Linden Press, 1985.

Ryan, Cornelius, and Kathryn Morgan Ryan. *A Private Battle*. New York: Fawcett Popular Library, 1979.

Selzer, Richard. *Raising the Dead: A Doctor's Encounter with His Own Mortality*. New York: Penguin Group, 1993.

Tanner, John. *Beating Back Pain*. London: Dorling Kinderley, 1987.

Practical
Basta, Lofty. *A Graceful Exit*. New York: Insight Books, 1996.

Bausell, R. Barker, Michael A. Rooney, and Charles Inlander. *How to Evaluate and Select A Nursing Home*. Reading, MA: Addison-Wesley, 1983.

Buckman, Robert, M.D. *How to Break Bad News: A Guide for Health Care Professionals*. Baltimore: The John Hopkins University Press, 1992.

Calahan, Daniel. *The Troubled Dream of Life: Living with Mortality*. New York: Simon and Schuster, 1993.

Covell, Mara. *The Home Alternative to Hospitals and Nursing Homes*. New York: Holt, Rinehart & Winston, 1983.

Doress, Paula Brown, Diana Laskin Siegal, et al. *Ourselves, Growing Older*. New York: Simon & Schuster, 1987.

Duda, Deborah. *Coming Home: A Guide to Dying at Home With Dignity*. New York: Aurora Press, 1987.

Feinstein, David and Peg Elliott Mayo. *Rituals for Living & Dying: How We Can Turn Loss & the Fear of Death into an Affirmation of Life*. San Francisco: Harper San Francisco, 1990.

Gamzales-Crussi, F. *The Day of the Dead and Other Mortal Reflections*. Orlando: Harcourt Brace and Co., 1993.

Hale, Glorya, ed. *The Source Book for the Disabled.* New York: Paddington, 1979.

Hill, Patrick T. and David Shirley. *A Good Death: Taking More Control at the End of Your Life.* Reading, MA: Addison-Wesley Publishing, 1992.

Hoefler, James. *Managing Death.* Boulder: Westview Press, 1997.

Kramer, Herbert and Kay. *Conversations at Midnight: Coming to Terms with Dying and Death.* New York: William Morrow & Company, 1993.

Lang, Susan S. and Richard B. Patt, M.D. *You Don't Have to Suffer: A Complete Guide to Relieving Cancer Pain for Patients and Their Families.* New York: Oxford University Press, 1994.

Larue, Gerald A. *Euthanasia & Religion: A Survey of the Attitudes of World Religions to the Right-to-Die.* Los Angeles: The Hemlock Society, 1985.

Levine, Stephen. *Healing into Life and Death.* New York: Doubleday, 1987.

Lifchez, Raymond, and Barbara Winslow. *Design for Independent Living: The Environment and Physically Disabled People.* Berkeley: University of California Press, 1979.

Lorimer, David. *Whole in One: The Near Death Experience and the Ethic of Interconnectedness.* New York: Penguin Group, 1990.

Nuland, Sherwin B. *How We Die: Reflections on Life's Final Chapter.* New York: Alfred A. Knopf, 1993.

Palmer, Greg. *The Trip of a Lifetime.* New York: HarperCollins, 1993.

Sankar, Andrea. *Dying At Home.* New York: Bantam Books, 1991.

Philosophical

Anthony, Nancy. *Mourning Thoughts: Facing a New Day After the Death of a Spouse.* Mystic, CT: Twenty-Third Publications, 1991.

Aries, Philippe. *The Hour of Our Death.* New York: Alfred A. Knopf, 1981.

Beauvoir, Simone de. *The Coming of Age.* New York: G.P. Putnam, 1972.

Becker, Ernest. *The Denial of Death.* New York: The Free Press, 1973.

Butler, Robert N. *Why Survive? Being Old in America.* New York: Harper & Row, 1975.

Enright, D.J., ed. *The Oxford Book of Death.* Oxford: Oxford Univ. Press, 1983.

Groopman, Jerome. *The Measure of Our Days.* New York: Viking Press, 1997.

Holbein, Hans. *The Dance of Death.* New York: Dover Press, 1971. (41 woodcuts originally published in 1538).

Keleman, Stanley. *Living Your Dying.* New York: Random House, 1974.

Krementz, Jill. *How It Feels When A Parent Dies.* New York: A. A. Knopf, 1981.

Kubler-Ross, Elizabeth. *On Death and Dying.* New York: Vintage Books, 1969.

Larue, Gerald A. *Euthanasia and Religion.* Los Angeles: Hemlock Society, 1985.

Levine, Stephen. *Who Dies?* New York: Anchor Books, 1982.

Lewis, C.S. *The Problem of Pain.* New York: Macmillan Publishing Co., 1974.

Mitford, Jessica. *The American Way of Death.* New York: Simon & Schuster, 1963.

Moody, Raymond. *Life After Life.* Harrisburg, PA: Stackpole Books, 1982.

Portwood, Doris. *Common Sense Suicide: The Final Right.* Los Angeles: The Hemlock Society, 1978.

Quill, Timothy E., M.D. *Death and Diginity: Making Choices and Taking Charge.* New York, London: W.W. Norton and Company, 1993.

Ross, Maggie. *Seasons of Death and Life: A Wilderness Memoir.*
San Francisco: Harper San Francisco, 1990.
Sharelson, Lonny. *A Chosen Death.* New York: Simon & Schuster, 1995.
Sivananda, Sri Swami. *What Becomes of the Soul After Death?* India: The
Divine Life Society, 1972.
Stoddard, Sandol. *The Hospice Movement.* New York: Vintage Books, 1978.
Taylor, Nick. *A Necessary End.* New York: Doubleday, 1994.
The Tibetan Book of the Dead.

Community Living
Theory
Bellamy Edward. *Looking Backward.* Boston: Houghton Mifflin, 1898.
Berneri, Marie Louise. *Journey Through Utopia.* Boston: Beacon Press, 1950.
Bookchin, Murray. *The Ecology of Freedom.* Palo Alto, CA: Cheshire, 1978.
Butler, Samuel. *Erewhon.* Edited by William Alfred Eddy. New York: T. Nelson
& Sons, 1930.
Callenbach, Ernest. *Ecotopia.* Berkeley: Banyan Tree Books, 1975.
————. *Ecotopia Emerging.* Berkeley: Banyan Tree Books, 1981.
Campanella, Tommaso. *City of the Sun.* Berkeley: Univ. of Calif. Press, 1981.
Cohen, Lottie, et al., ed. *Cooperative Housing Compendium.* Davis, GA:
Center for Cooperatives, 1993.
Driver, Tom F. *The Magic of Ritual.* San Francisco: Harpers, 1991.
Ehrenhalt, Alan. *The Lost City.* New York: Bask Books, 1995.
Fourier, Charles. *Design for Utopia.* New York: Schocken Press.
Goodman, Paul, and Percival Goodman. *Communitas.* New York: Vintage, 1960.
Hanson, Claus. *The Cohousing Handbook.* Port Robert's, WA: Hartley and
Marks Publishers, 1996.
Hinds, William A. *American Communities and Cooperative Colonies.* Chicago:
Porcupine Press, 1975.
Kanter, Rosebeth Moss. *Commitment and Community.* Cambridge: Harvard
University Press, 1972.
Kilpatrick, Joseph. *Better Than Money Can Buy.* Winston-Salem: Inner
Search Publishing, 1995.
Kriyananda, Swami. *Cooperative Communities.* Ananda Publications.
Kropotkin, Peter. *Mutual Aid.* Boston: Extending Horizon Books, 1955.
Lasky, Melvin. *Utopia and Revolution.* Chicago: Univ, of Chicago Press, 1976.
LeGuin, Ursula. *The Dispossessed.* New York: Harper & Row, 1974.
Mannheim, Karl. *Ideology & Utopia.* New York: Harcourt, Brace, World, 1953.
Manuel, Frank, and Fritze Manuel. *Utopian Thought in the Western World.*
Cambridge, MA: Harvard University Press, 1979.
McNeill, William H. *Keeping Together in Time.* Cambridge: Harvard University
Press, 1995.
More, Sir Thomas. *Utopia.* Edited by J. Rawson Lumby. Cambridge: Cambridge
University Press, 1956.
Morehouse, Ward, ed. *Building Sustainable Communities.* New York: The
Bootstrap Press, 1989.

Morris, William. *Escape from Nowhere*. International Publishers.

Norwood, Ken, and Kathleen Smith. *Building Community in America*. Berkeley: Shared Living Resource Center, 1995.

Nozick, Robert. *Anarchy, State and Utopia*. New York: Basic Books, 1974.

Peck, Scott M. *The Different Drum: Community-Making and Peace*. New York: Simon and Schuster, 1987.

Plato. *Republic*. Edited and translated by I. A. Richards. Cambridge: Cambridge University Press, 1966.

Shaffer, Carolyn R., and Kristen Anundsen. *Creating Community Anywhere*. New York: G. P. Putnam's Sons, 1993.

Skinner, B. F. *Walden Two*. London: Macmillan, 1948.

Tod, Ian, and Michael Wheeler. *Utopia*. Glendale, CA: Crown Publishers, 1978.

Vanier, Jean. *Community and Growth*. Mahwah, NJ: Paulist Press, 1979.

Veysey, Laurence. *The Communal Experience*. New York: Harper & Row, 1973.

Walter, Bob, et. al., ed. *Sustainable Cities*. Los Angeles: Eco-Home Media, 1992.

Wells, H. G. *A Modern Utopia*. Lincoln, Nebr.: Univ. of Nebraska Press, 1967.

White, Frederic Randolph. *Famous Utopias of the Renaissance*. New York: Hendricks House, 1955.

Williamson, Scott, G., and Innes Pearse. *Science, Synthesis and Sanity*. Edinburgh: Scottish Academic Press, 1980.

____. *Ecotopia Revisited*. Kanter, Rosebeth Moss. *Commitment and Community*. Cambridge, MA: Harvard University Press, 1972.

Practice

Andrews, Edward. *The People Called Shakers*. New York: Dover Books, 1970.

Arnold, Emmy. *Torches Together: The Story of the Bruderhof Communities*. Rifton, N.Y.: Plough Publishing House, 1964.

Autobiography of Brook Farm. New York: Prentice Hall, Inc.

Beame, Hugh, et al. *Home Comfort: Stories and Scenes of Life on Total Loss Farm*. New York: Saturday Review Books, 1973.

Bens mann, Dieter, et al. *Das Kommune Pouch*. Göttinger: Verlag Die Werkstatt, 1996.

Burkowitz, Bob. *Local Heroes*. Lexington, Mass.: Lexington Books, 1987.

Das Europäische Projekte—Verzeichnis 97/98. *Eurotopia: Leben in Gemeinschaft*. Beinin: Bezug: Eurotopia, 1997.

Duberman, Martin. *Black Mountain*. New York: E. P. Dutton, 1972.

Fairfield, Richard. *Communes USA: A Personal Tour*. Baltimore: Penguin, 1972.

Fitzgerald, Frances. *Cities on a Hill*. New York: Simon and Schuster, 1986.

Fogarty, Robert. *The Righteous Remnant*. Kent, Ohio: Kent State Univ., 1981.

Gaskin, Stephen. *Volume One*. The Book Publ. Co., Summertown, TN 38483.

Gravy, Wavy. *The Hog Farm*. Links Books.

Haggard, Ben. *Living Community: A Permaculture Case Study*. Santa Fe: Sol y Sombra Foundation, 1993.

Hermann, Janet Sharp. *The Pursuit of a Dream*. New York: Oxford Univ., 1981.

Hine, Robert. *California's Utopian Colonies*. Berkeley: University of California Press, 1953.

Holloway, Mark. *Heavens on Earth: Utopian Communities in America 1680–1880*. New York: Dover Books, 1951.

Hostetler, John. *Amish Society*. Baltimore: Johns Hopkins Press, 1968.

Houriet, Robert. *Getting Back Together*. New York: Coward, McCann & Geoghegan, 1971.

Institute for Community Economics. *The Community Land Trust Handbook*. Emmaus, PA: Rodale Press, 1982.

Interaction Member Profiles 1993. Washington D.C.: Interaction, 1993.

Janzen, David. *Fire, Salt & Peace: Intentional Christian Communities Alive in North America*. Evanston Il.: Shalom Mission Communities Press, 1996.

Kagan, Paul. *New World Utopias*. New York: Penguin Books, 1975.

Kerista Commune. *Kerista*. Performing Arts Social Society, 1984.

Kinkade, Kathleen. *A Walden Two Experiment*. New York: William Morrow, 1973.

Kinkade, Kat. *Is It Utopia Yet?* Louisa, VA: Twin Oaks Press, 1994.

Kipps, Harriet Clyde, ed. *Volunteerism: The Directory of Organizations, Training, Programs and Publications*. New Providence, New Jersey: R.R. Bowker, 1991.

Komar, Ingrid. *Living the Dream* (Twin Oaks Community), Norwood Editions.

Krishna, Anirudh, ed. *Reasons for Hope: Instructional Experiences in Rural Development*. West Hartford: Kumarian Press, 1997.

Lee, Dallas. *The Cotton Patch Evidence*. New York: Harper & Row, 1971.

Lockwood, George. *The New Harmony Movement*. New York: Appleton, 1905.

MacCarthy, Fiona. *The Simple Life, C.R. Ashbee in the Cotswolds*. Berkeley: University of California Press, 1981.

McCamant, Kathryn, and Charles Durett. *Cohousing—A Contemporary Way of Housing Ourselves*. Berkeley: Ten Speed Press, 1988.

McKee, Rose. *Brother Will and the Founding of Gould Farm*. W. J. Gould, 1963.

McLaughlin, Corinne and Gordon Davidson. *Builders of the Dawn*. Walpole, N.H.: Stillpoint Press, 1985.

Metcalf, Bill. *From Utipian Dreaming to Communal Reality: Cooperative Lifestyles in Australia*. Sydney: UNSW Press, 1995.

Melville, Keith. *Communes in the Counter Culture*. New York: W. Morrow, 1972.

Mintz, Jerry, Raymond and Sidney Solomon. *The Handbook of Alternative Education*. New York: MacMillan Publishing Co., 1994.

Nordhoff, Charles. *The Communistic Societies of the United States*. New York: Schocken Books, 1965.

Noyes, John Humphrey. *Strange Cults and Utopias of 19th Century America*. New York: Dover Books, 1969.

Pearse, Innes H. *The Peckham Experiment*. London: Allen & Unwin, 1943.

Peters, Victor. *All Things Common, The Hutterite Way of Life*. Minneapolis: University of Minnesota Press, 1965.

Pitzer, Donald, ed. *America's Communal Utopias*. Chapel Hill: The University of North Carolina Press, 1997.

Shearer, Ann. *L'Arche*. St. Paul, MN: Daybreak Press, 1975.

Spiro, Melford. *Kibbutz: Venture in Utopia*. New York: Schocken Books, 1970.

Sundancer, Elaine. *Celery Wine: Story of a Country Commune*. Community Publications Cooperative, 1973.

Taylor, James B. *Mary's City of David.* Benton Harbor, MI: Mary's City of David Publishing, 1996.

Weisbrod, Carol. *The Boundaries of Utopia.* New York: Pantheon Books, 1980.

Whyte, William, and Kathleen Whyte. *Making Mondragon.* New York: Cornell University Press, 1988.

Williams, Paul. *Apple Bay.* New York: Warner Books.

Yablonsky, Lewis. *Synanon.* Baltimore: Pelican Books, 1965.

Zablocki, Benjamin. *The Joyful Community.* Baltimore: Penguin Books, 1971.

Periodicals

Building Economic Alternatives. Coop America. 2100 M Street, N.W. Washington, DC 20063.

Camphill Soltane. 224 Nantmeal Road, Glenmore, PA 19343.

Cohousing Network. 1705 14th St. #160, Boulder, CO 80302.

Communal Societies. Center for Communal Studies, Univ. of S. Indiana, Evansville, IN 47712.

Communes At Large Letter. ICD (Yaakov Setter), Yad Tabenkin, Ramat Efal 42960 Israel.

Communities—A Journal of Cooperative Learning. 105 Sunset Street, Stelle, IL 60919.

Kerista: Journal of Utopian Group Living. Kerista Publications/Performing Arts Society.

Leaves of Twin Oaks. Twin Oaks Community, 138 Twin Oaks Rd., Louisa, VA 23093.

New Opinions. Mark Satin, Editor. 2005 Massachussetts Ave., N.W. Washington, DC 20063

One Earth. Findhorn Community, The Park, Findhorn, Forres IU36 OT2, Scotland, U.K.

Permaculture Activist. P.O. Box 1209, Black Mountain, N.C. 28711.

The Plough. Publication of Bruderhof Community, Spring Valley Bruderhoff, Farmington, PA 15437.

Whole Earth Review. P.O. Box 38, Sausalito, CA 94966.

Directories

A Guide to Cooperative Alternatives. Community Publications Cooperative. 105 Sun Street, Steele, Il 60919.

Alternative Communities. The Teachers. 18 Garth Road, Bangor Gwynedd, North Wales.

New Age Directory. Victor Kulvinskas. Omangod Press.

Art as Therapy

Csikszentmihalyi, Mihaly. *Flow: the Psychology of Optimal Experience.* New York: Harper and Row, 1990.

Dewey, John. *Art As Experience.* New York: Capricorn Books, 1934.

Koestler, Arthur. *The Art of Creation.* New York: Macmillan, 1964.

May, Rollo. *The Courage To Create.* New York: Bantam Books, 1975.

Nachmanovitch, Stephen. *Free Play.* Los Angeles: Jeremy Tarcher, 1990.

Oech, Roger von. *A Kick in the Seat of the Pants*. New York: Perennial Library, 1986.

———. *A Whack on the Side of the Head*. New York: Warner Books, 1983.

Organizations

International Arts in Medicine Association
19 South 22nd Street
Philadelphia, PA 19103

National Coalition of Arts Therapy Associations
505 11th Street, S.E.
Washington, D.C. 20003
(202) 543-6864

International Society for Music for Medicine
Paulmannshoher Strasse
17D-5880 Ludenscheid, Germany

HEALTH RESOURCES

Publications & Organizations
Alternative & Complementary Therapies
Mary Ann Liebert
2 Madison Avenue
Larchmont, NY 10538

Alternative Therapies
101 Columbia
Aliso Viejo, CA 92656

American Assn. of Naturopathic Physicians
2366 Eastlake Ave. E., Suite 322
Seattle, WA 98102

Audobon
P.O. Box 52529
Boulder, CO 80322

Back Pain Assn. of America
P.O. Box 135
Pasadena, CA 21123

Dendron News
for Psychiatric Survivors
454 Willamette St., Suite 216
P.O. Box 11284
Eugene, OR 97440

Diabetes Wellness Newsletter
P.O. Box 231
Shrub Oak, NY 10588

Earthstewards Network
P.O. Box 10697
Bainbridge Island, WA 98110

Emotional Anonymous
P.O. Box 4245
St. Paul, MN 55104

Epilepsy Foundation of America
4351 Garden City Dr.
Landover, MD 20785

Friends of Peace Pilgrim
43480 Cedar Avenue
Hemet, CA 92544

Giraffe Project
P.O. Box 759, 197 2nd St.
Langley, WA 98260

Habitat For Humanity
121 Habitat St.
Americus, GA 31709

The Herbalist
American Herbalists' Guild
P.O. Box 1683
Soquel, CA 95073

Herbclip
American Botanical Council
P.O. Box 201660
Austin, TX 78720

Hesperian Foundation
P.O. Box 11577
Berkeley, CA 94712

Hope
P.O. Box 160, Naskeag Rd.
Brooklin, ME 04616

Human Kindness Foundation
Rt. 1 Box 201-N
Durham, NC 27705

Human Service Alliance
3983 Old Greensboro Rd.
Winston-Salem, NC 27101

Interaction Member Profiles 1993
1993 Directory of Service Org.
American Council for Voluntary
International Action
1717 Massachusetts Avenue, N.W.
Washington, D.C. 20036

Kipps, Harnet C. *Volunteerism:
The Directory of Organizations*
New Providence, New Jersey:
Reed Publishing, 1991.

*Journal of Alternative &
Complementary Medicine*
Mary Ann Liebert
2 Madison Avenue
Larchmont, NY 10538

Medical Acupuncture
American Acad. of Medical Acupuncture
5820 Wilshire Blvd., Suite 500
Los Angeles, CA 90036

Meridians
Traditional Acupuncture Institute
American City Building
10227 Wincopin Circle, Suite 100
Columbia, MD 21044

Mood Disorder Support Group
Box 1747 Madison Square Station
New York, NY 10159

National Assn. of Psychiatric Survivors
P.O. Box 618
Sioux Falls, SD 57101

National Chronic Pain Association
7979 Old Georgetown Road, Suite 100
Bethesda, MD 20814

National Foundation for the
Chemically Hypersensitive
P.O. Box 70844
Washington, D.C. 20024

Natural History
Central Park at 79th St.
New York, N.Y. 10024

Natural Wildlife Magazine
8925 Leesburg Pike
Vienna, VA 22184

Natural Health
17 Station St.
Brookline, MA 02146

Network
The Scientific & Medical Network Review
Gibliston Mill
Colinsburgh
Leven, Fife
Scotland KY9 1JS U.K.

Obsessive-Compulsive Anonymous
P.O. Box 215
New Hyde Park, NY 11040

Obsessive-Compulsive Foundation
P.O. Box 70
Milford, CT 06460

Options (Journal) Resource of
volunteer opportunities for
health care professionals
Project Concern International
3550 Afton Road
San Diego, CA 92123

Physicians' Association of
Anthroposophic Medicine
*Journal of Anthroposophic
Medicine*
7953 California Avenue
Fair Oaks, CA 95628

Positive News & Living Lightly
The Six Bells
Bishop's Castle
Shropshire SY9 SAA, England

Prevention Magazine
P.O. Box 7319
Red Oak, IA 51591

Resurgence (Ecology/Spirituality)
Rocksea Farmhouse
St. Mabyn, Bodinn
Cornwall PL30 3BR England

Spirit At Work
36 Sylvan Hills Rd.
East Haven, CT 03513

Talking Leaves /Global Journal
on Spiritual Ecology & Activism
1511 K St. N.W., Suite 412
Washington, D.C. 20005

Whole Earth
P.O. Box 3000
Denville, NJ 07834

World Goodwill
3 Whitehall Court Suite 59
London 5eW1A 2EF, U.K.

Yes: Journal of Positive Futures
P.O. Box 10818
Bainbridge Island, WA 98110

About the Cartoonist

Jerry Van Amerongen grew up on Ballard Street in Grand Rapids, Michigan. Women in large print dresses and droopy lidded men in baggy trousers—all of them caught up in unfathomable behavior and homemade contraptions—are the folks from his childhood who have appeared in his cartooning ever since.

From 1980 to 1990 Van Amerongen graced the comic pages of newspapers across the country with his zany revolutionary cartoon panel, THE NEIGHBORHOOD. He, along with Gary Larson and THE FAR SIDE, redefined the single panel gag cartoon with their single shot doses of absurdity, providing a more sophisticated and surreal sense of humor.

In 1990, for principally creative reasons, Van Amerongen stopped drawing The Neighborhood and began BALLARD STREET, in strip form. After the first two years, the Ballard Street strip was slowly moved back to a panel, which seems to be his natural voice. Ballard Street is presently carried in 100 papers nationwide.

A new Ballard Street book collection, titled *Ballard Street: New from the creator of The Neighborhood* (1998), is available from Andrews McMeel Publishing, an Andrews McMeel Universal company, 4520 Main Street, Kansas City, Missouri 64111. Their website is: www.andrewsmcmeel.com.

Ballard Street greeting cards, calendars, mugs, stationery, and T-shirts are also in distribution. To see more of Jerry's work, visit his syndicate's website: www.creators.com.

About the Author

Patch Adams, M.D. is the founder/director of the Gesundheit Institute, a twenty-seven year old project to create a hospital that addresses all the problems of care delivery. They have never charged money, accepted third party reimbursement, or carried malpractice insurance. It is the first hospital to fully integrate all the healing arts and to be wellness and arts focused. The hospital is home to staff and patients. It is the first "silly" hospital in history and under construction now as an ecovillage.

Patch has been a clown for over thirty years, performing all over the world and taking a group of clowns every year (for eleven years) to Russia.

He is the author of *Gesundheit* (Healing Arts Press), which has been made into the movie "Patch Adams" by Universal Pictures (Release date: December 1998). It stars Robin Williams as Patch.

At his core, Patch is a political activist, desiring a world that has replaced the gods of greed and power with generosity and compassion. He is a lover of poetry, dance, nature, people, and service. His two precious treasures are his sons, Zag and Lars.

Books Available From Robert D. Reed Publishers

Please include payment with orders. Send indicated book/s to:

Name:_____

Address:_____

City:_____ State:_____ Zip:_____

Phone:(____)_____Fax:_____ E-mail:_____

Book Title	Unit Price	Qty.	Sub-total
House Calls: How we can all heal the world one visit at a time by Patch Adams, M.D.	$11.95	____	_____
500 Tips For Coping With Chronic Illness by Pamela D. Jacobs, M.A.	11.95	____	_____
Coping With Your Child's Chronic Illness by Alesia T. Barrett Singer, M.A.	9.95	____	_____
Healing Is Remembering Who You Are by Marilyn Gordon (hypnotherapist)	11.95	____	_____
Lovers & Survivors: A Partner's Guide To Living With & Loving A Sexual Abuse Survivor by S.Y. de Beixedon, Ph.D.	14.95	____	_____
Super Kids In 30 Minutes A Day by Karen U. Kwiatkowski, M.S., M.A.	9.95	____	_____
50 Things You Can Do About Guns by James M. Murray	7.95	____	_____
Get Out Of Your Thinking Box by Lindsay Collier	7.95	____	_____
Healing Our Schools by S. P. Mitchell	11.95	____	_____
The Funeral Book by C.W. Miller	7.95	____	_____
Live To Be 100+ by Richard G. Deeb	11.95	____	_____

Enclose a copy of this order form and payment for books. Send to address below. Shipping & handling: $2.50 for first book and $1.00 for each additional book. California residents please add 8.5% sales tax. Discounts for large orders. Please make checks payable to the publisher: Robert D. Reed. Total enclosed: $_____.

Send orders to or contact publisher for more information:
Robert D. Reed Publishers
750 La Playa, Suite 647 • San Francisco, CA 94121
Phone: 650/994-6570 • Fax: 650/994-6579
Email: 4bobreed@msn.com • http://www.rdrpublishers.com